Students As Real People

*Interpersonal Communication
and Education*

Students As Real People

Interpersonal Communication and Education

ROB ANDERSON

Southern Illinois University Edwardsville

LONDON AND NEW YORK

To Dona, Eric, and Neil—
my most helpful learning community

First published 1979 by Hayden Book Company, Inc.

Published 2019 by Routledge
2 Park Square, Milton Park, Abingdon, Oxon, OX14 4RN
52 Vanderbilt Avenue, New York, NY 10017

First issued in hardback 2019

Routledge is an imprint of the Taylor & Francis Group, an informa business

Copyright © 1979 by Taylor & Francis.

All rights reserved. No part of this book may be reprinted or reproduced or utilised in any form or by any electronic, mechanical, or other means, now known or hereafter invented, including photocopying and recording, or in any information storage or retrieval system, without permission in writing from the publishers.

Notice:
Product or corporate names may be trademarks or registered trademarks, and are used only for identification and explanation without intent to infringe.

Library of Congress Cataloging in Publication Data

Anderson, Robert Orlie, 1945–
   Students as real people.

   Includes index.
   1. Interaction analysis in education.
2. Communication in education. 3. College
students—Psychology. I. Title.
LB3609.A53   301.5′6   78-11978
ISBN 0-8104-5764-4

ISBN 13: 978-1-138-53364-6 (hbk)
ISBN 13: 978-0-8104-5764-5 (pbk)

preface

It is July 1977, and I'm preparing the final version of the manuscript. I'm sad—sad and relieved. It feels good to create a sort of closure, even if I seem only artificially "finished." But planning my message for student communicators has taken a lot of my energy for several years, and I will deeply miss my involvement in this writing. Perhaps the size of the book doesn't indicate how much *Students As Real People* has been with me—in my mind, on scratch paper, in classes, in daydreams. It hurts a bit to let it go.

But (I tell myself) true sharing doesn't involve letting anything *go*. I'm not diminished by letting someone else see my vision; I still have it. No book really exists on paper. I may find that you already hold a similar vision, which will be affirming for me. Or I may glimpse your dissimilar vision, and be affirmed in a different way. Anyway, I welcome and anticipate your sharing of reactions to the book. You can contact me by writing to the Department of Speech Communication, Southern Illinois University at Edwardsville, Edwardsville, Illinois 62026.

I feel warm gratitude toward many people who have sustained and supported this project. My family teaches me always—parents, wife, and sons. To students in my classes I owe the insight that only real people can learn. Several of them—Kay Firsching, Bill Freeman, and Beth Rodgers—served as informal reviewers of this book, and their reactions were always important to me. My special friends in various TORI groups (see Chapter 5) and at the La Jolla Program of the Center for Studies of the Person helped me learn about community and personal growth potential. My colleagues at SIUE—Pat Goehe, Annette Graebe, Bob Hawkins, Joe Munshaw, Dan Salden, Richard Stoppe, and Dave Valley— have worked hard to create a department in which authentic learning can happen; I continue to value them. At a time when I doubted I could write a book, I was bolstered by the faith of Ted Shields, whose venture, Shields Publishing Company, now persists in spirit only. And, finally, I appreciate the help of editors and reviewers at Hayden, who consistently encouraged my writing to be *my* writing.

Rob Anderson

contents

1. COMMUNICATING AT COLLEGE   1
   Stimulus for the Book 1
   Student Audiences 3
   What the Book Is and Is Not 3

2. ARE STUDENTS PERSONS?   6
   The Concept of Person 8
   American Education and Its
      Expectations of Students 14
   Why This Book Is about
      Interpersonal Communication 20

3. EDUCATION AS COMMUNICATION   22
   Considering Interpersonal Communication 23
   Learning, Caring, and Other Educational Matters 34
   Alternative Models of Educational Responsibility:
      A Summary 39

4. LISTENING AS OTHER-AFFIRMATION   41
   A Personal Note 42
   Functions of Listening Behavior 43
   Affirming 45
   Listening and Student Culture 49

5. HONEST MESSAGES AS OTHER-AFFIRMATION   54
   (R)Evolution 54
   Affirming by Trust 56
   Openness: Both Ways 59
   (R)Evolution and Change 71

6. THE ECOLOGY OF ACADEMIC AUDIENCES   73
   Our Audienceness 73
   The Importance of Understanding Audience 74

Campus Relationships: I Am a System, You Are a System,
We Are a System 75
Synergy 76
Ecology 79
You as Teachers' Audience, Teachers
as Your Audience 87
The Future of an Ecology of Audiences 91

7. ACTION, REACTION, AND INACTION IN
HIGHER EDUCATION   93
Dear Student . . . 93
Doing 95
Action Alternatives 95
P. S. . . . 116

APPENDICES   118
Appendix A (1975) 119
Appendix B (1976) 121
Appendix C (1977) 124

INDEX   130

prologue

There are many good things in Rob Anderson's book, not the least of which is the rare clarity of his writing. I wish we'd had a Rob Anderson in our department when I was an undergraduate speech major. I wish we'd had his text.

"What does a speech major do?" people would ask me when they heard what I was taking.

"I don't know; speak, I guess." Maybe a speech major could teach speech. But I didn't want to become a lecturer. I didn't know about this other way of teaching, the way Rob seems to have invented, treating teaching and learning as building honest relationships in the classroom.

Not wanting to teach, I became a psychologist. I was hungry for relationships, and I thought I could find them through becoming a psychotherapist. That worked, but the best relationships I found were at home.

Relating is loving, and the easiest people to love (and probably those who need it most) are those who are right under your nose, those you live with. I say "easiest," but that's not quite true. You get used to the people in your family. They don't seem as remarkable or attractive as strangers. In that sense, it's easier to love strangers (hence the popularity of serial relating, divorce, etc.). But when you really love someone, you want to take them home with you. In that sense it's easier to love your family. You don't have to take them home with you. They're already there. But you have to notice them! You have to pay attention!

I envy you the class you're embarking on. If you really get Rob's message, you're going to have a wonderful semester. You're going to let yourself be known. It's a rare opportunity: to feel that another person, or a valued group, really knows you. I hope you go home and do the same for your family. Let them know you. It'll turn out to be identical to knowing them. In relationship, knowing and being known are part of the same process. They meet in the middle.

I want to tell you about the time I noticed my seven-year-old daughter. Noticing her taught me something I often forget: how lucky I am to live with real, live human persons. And it taught me something about the relationship and communication: that sometimes it won't do to demand that the other person become her better self; you have to take the first risk yourself.

Elizabeth was mad. She stormed around the kitchen table, screaming about a *papier-mâché* mask she needed for a first-grade project. She wanted to form it by laying moistened paper towels over a balloon. Each time she smoothed on a new towel, the others wrinkled and slipped.

Mother was making dinner and couldn't help. Jane our teenager, who sometimes can handle Elizabeth, had gotten mad herself and given up.

"Won't somebody help me? I can't do it. I'm not old enough—AUGGH!" Another towel had slipped.

Eleven-year-old John spoke up. "Nobody wants to help you, Beth, because you holler at them." This was a reasonable thing for John to say, but Elizabeth was crying too loudly to hear.

I made a psychological analysis. "She's pretty upset," I said. I went into the living room. I faced a decision. I could read the evening paper and shut out the noise. Parents of young children develop skill at shutting out noise. Or I could go back to the kitchen and shut up Elizabeth. I could throw the balloon and towels away and put Elizabeth in her room until she realized how to act like a decent person.

What to do with a little girl? How best to raise one? I get confused. But could I reverse the problem and find an answer? Could I ask what sort of person I wanted to be?

I could. And then I knew I didn't want to be the avenger, saying "I'll teach you to cry!" And I knew I didn't want to be a coward, hiding in my paper. Instead I remembered that I hadn't held my little girl on my lap in a long time, though I had held my newspaper nightly.

I called Elizabeth into the living room and asked if she would sit on my lap. She did, and she cried and I felt good because I was holding a little human being in my arms. Soon she would be a big human being and it would be more awkward to hold her.

I remembered, too, the lesson of our family meetings, which is that young people are sensible to one another and caring when you give them the right opportunity. I asked John if he would come in.

"John, you used to have a problem with crying, didn't you? I remember that the children used to tease you and call you a crybaby."

"Yes."

"But you stopped. Do you remember when you stopped or how you managed?"

"I was about six. I don't remember why I stopped. I know I got tired of the teasing. I guess I just grew up."

I didn't really think John could advise Elizabeth. She is in a phase. There are signs she is growing out of it already. But I had to note that by the time John and I had finished talking, Elizabeth had finished crying. That was good—a bonus. What was best, however, was that three people who didn't have to be were in a room together. They lived together and often didn't notice. Now they were paying attention.

One of them, eleven years old, spoke softly of himself and of what it had been like to be six.

One of them, just turned seven, lay in her daddy's arms and cried quietly, which sure beats screaming.

And one of them was pleased to be a father.

Dr. Bill Coulson
Center for Studies of the Person
La Jolla, California

1

communicating at college

Stimulus for the Book

As I look over my shoulder at my not-too-distant undergraduate years in college, I can't escape the conclusion that I cheated myself out of a great deal of education that was rightfully mine. It's not easy to cheat yourself; it takes quite a bit of perseverance and outright work. This did not stand in my way, for like many in the American system of education, I was long on virtues like perseverance, work, patience, and consistency, but pretty short on exuberance, joy, emotional involvement, interaction, and above all, a sense of power and importance.

Actually, I concentrated on being a "good student," submerging my humanness into a role, fearing communication of any depth in my educational environment. That was the source of my cheating myself, and that is the principal stimulus for what you are reading now—an attempt to encourage you to relate to my personal frustrations and fun in education as well as my hopes for what it can become.

I gave in so consistently to the traditional niceties of college life that I became a semiperson, convinced that the classroom was no place to interact, but to receive; no place to display or empathize with emotion, but to take notes; no place to do, but to hear of what others have done. I usually let myself be isolated from contacts with anyone other than my narrow clique of friends, and let myself be intimidated by more than a few instructors.

My personal inaction and academic impotence interacted with the system of expectations—norms and roles— in which I found myself. By and large, higher education has discouraged communication among students, and, in fact, among all subcommunities of academic culture. It has seemingly defined its salvation as the depersonalization of the learning

students as real people

process, as the heightening of the mythical ideal of "objectivity," as the ritualization of student-student, student-faculty, and student-administrator relationships.

Just as I was socialized into the miniature society of family in my youth, learning quickly which actions I could get away with and which led to closed doors and denied privileges, I was socialized in college to develop an incredible respect for Information (I could be rewarded by memorizing and later forgetting it) and a disregard and/or contempt for relationships (I was told by the demands of my environment that the development of them is "inefficient," and sometimes punishable). Instead of being rewarded for being a good communicator, I found myself most highly rewarded when I removed part of myself from my campus interactions with others, when I inhibited emotional reactions, when I was the most phony, when I avoided personal relationships with significant students and teachers. Thus I had more time to study and in other ways forget what school really should be about. I now realize that studying should be a response to internal stimuli; when it is not, it becomes social camouflage for scared, lonely, disguised, and closed people.

My purpose is not to lash wildly at the grading system. It is probably only symptomatic of a more deeply-rooted communication disease. But students and teachers too often let grades become a powerful two-directional barrier to meaningful communication. Even if you aren't a Dean's List student, you may have some identification with Brian McGuire's college experience. He graduated one year with the highest grade average in the University of California, Berkeley's College of Letters and Science. Despite this achievement, he told his fellow students publicly that ". . . it was not worth it," and that "my compulsive effort for a high grade point in my years at Berkeley contributed to an almost total alienation of myself from other people." For the model student image, Brian McGuire traded "participat[ion] in the values of the societies around me," and "human bonds with my fellow students."[1] Though I retain a grudging admiration for "good students," I admire good communicators more, and can't understand why the categories have to be mutually exclusive.

My real concern in writing this book is for thousands who are cheating themselves in their education in almost precisely the same ways I cheated myself in mine some years ago. I see myself so painfully reflected in them that I want to make explicit some connections I see between my experience and theirs.

---

[1] McGuire's speech is reprinted in Mary Greer and Bonnie Rubinstein, *Will the Real Teacher Please Stand Up? A Primer in Humanistic Education* (Pacific Palisades, California: Goodyear, 1972), p. 28.

communicating at college

Student Audiences

I have written with the undergraduate student in mind, whether at large universities or small colleges, four year or community colleges, public or private schools, residential or commuter campuses. Though differences are apparent, so many of the same institutional demands and potential responses apply to all these environments that the American college student could well feel a profound sense of community with his or her colleagues in learning. That there is demonstrably no such feeling is evidence of one of the most persistent communication problems administrators and faculty face in higher education—how to encourage students to realize that their education is something *other students* can help them develop.

You may well be reading this book in connection with an introductory course in interpersonal communication. Any course in communication must draw on some basic conceptual insights and explore possibilities for the application of concepts. But what kind of application? In my experience, the thing that often interests college students the most is simply being college students. I discover in my classes that students in the main care strongly about their own education and are willing—and often irrepressively anxious—to discuss it, and participate actively in it. What better arena, then, to seek applications for the communication concepts you learn? Your years in college could be one of the most meaningful times in your life, or they could be in retrospect a bad dream of missed opportunities, unfounded fears, and memories of powerlessness. The difference is in the relationships you form or fail to form with others; the difference is in communication.

Therefore, I'm hoping my writing might be useful also for teacher education programs, study skills courses, workshops in educational communication, or the general reader interested in higher education. I feel in-harmony with the gathering momentum of humanistic educational thought which treats education as a self-directed process, teaching as facilitation, emotional growth as a coequal and intermeshed goal with cognitive growth, and learning as an activity rather than a passivity. Perhaps my central message is that everything anyone does in the educational system may be understood as communication.

What the Book Is and Is Not

You can develop the habit of discussing American higher education as a communication environment with an ecology all its own. Perhaps you consider yourself an important natural resource in that environment already. I hope so, and congratulations are in order if that is

students as real people

you. But so many students do not that I'm tempted to write primarily with them in mind, and write consciously and subjectively from my own experience because of empathy for their frustration.

Students As Real People is my attempt to contribute to the development of your own personal philosophies of communication and education. I am weary—and wary—of books and people trying to teach me; I welcome those that seem to want to let me learn. The distinction matters. I see in myself (and many others) a constant curiosity about those parts of the outside world that affect me most deeply. I learn things when it is fun and/or necessary to do so through the production and direction of my own curiosity. I don't learn by pressing some "on-off" button which activates my brain. Nor do I learn when someone else seems to assume I have that button and they are in control of it. Our best learnings do not take place when we are working as subordinates in the control of a leader, but when we are satisfying an internal voice stating "This is important. I'll be better off if I learn this." Maybe you don't recognize much of this latter brand of learning in your past formal education. If so, you have something to strive for.

Consequently, I refuse to add to the mountain of books supplying *answers*. At first consideration, this may sound unusual for student-directed writing. For what, in the popular mind, are students if not answer-receivers? But answers are highly individualized items. Chances are, if you ask the right questions, you will find your own answers, whether someone else tries to push theirs off on you or not. Certainly I have no mandate to package Truth, and you shouldn't let me even if I could. The study of communication leads to no conclusion faster than the realization of inescapable relativity in the world. What I can package, though, and hope you are curious about, is *a* truth; a kind of anthology of personal observations of mine and others which seem to be true from my perspective. You will perceive the questions I ask myself about communication and education. You will perceive the directions in which I am moving and hopefully compare them to your directions. In a sense, this is a workbook without the coercion or the blanks, because you are responsible for "filling in the answers" merely by noticing personal applications in your specific situation.

You may already understand that writing books for students is a risky business. It has not been too long since I was a student, and can therefore remember the disdain with which I treated most of the texts, because they were just texts. I made fun of authors, jokingly wondering if they were human or just typewriters set on automatic pilot. Did they have *lives*? Did they shoot baskets, brush dogs, wake up with headaches, and use tissues to blow their noses? I never really found out, because they didn't collaborate with me in communication. They treated commu-

4

communicating at college

nication as a one-way supply of answers rather than the interdependent efforts of people in a relationship to generate common meaning.

Here I have to depend so much on your collaboration that you may ultimately snicker at these words as derisively as I did those other books which seemed so alien, clinical, remote, and impersonal. That's a major fear of mine. But I've decided to adopt the tone of *writing you a letter*, as much as that is possible. My decision may be meaningful for you; it may not. The whole concept of being personal in an academic book may seem ludicrous and unnecessary to some people. But there are risks in almost everything important, aren't there? So I'll take my chances.

2

are
students
persons?

I feel slightly uneasy asking if students are persons. You don't know me well enough to know how I like to use the word "person," and I suspect you might use it differently. You might use it to denote any member of our species, in which case the question is clearly dumb; "of course students are people," you could validly respond from your frame of reference, "what else?"

But I have another question which may serve to clarify my intentions.

What should your teachers teach? If you answer (and suspect they'd answer) "History," "English," "Political Science," "Physics," "Speech Communication," etc., consider this chapter carefully. You may be operating in a system in which you are not a person at all; in which the answer to the question posed in my title is not as obvious as it might initially seem. Calling students people doesn't make it so, especially when no one acts as if it were true. Although I sometimes lapse into equally misleading verbal shorthand, I have to ask the question again and hope that this second answer makes more sense to you.

What should your teachers teach? People. That is, they should work alongside and cooperatively with human beings who, if they decide to, can become full participants in the process of education, fully human, persons in the fullest, and I think the only meaningful, sense of the word. You are not automatically a person. You begin to become a person only (1) if you have begun to recognize and act in consonance with your unique capabilities as a human, and (2) if significant, others in your environment recognize your uniqueness and take you into account. It isn't difficult to observe whether these things are happening in your life and in your role as a student. Communication is your clue. Listen to your messages being transmitted to others. And, equally important, listen to what others think of you as reflected in their messages.

6

are students persons?

You can often identify your friends, because in listening to them you see that they take you into account; you see that you are important to them in unique ways, ways which stimulate caring and mutual commitment. And, conversely, you can identify those to whom you are a nonperson, even though you also interact with them in a variety of verbal and nonverbal contexts. Erving Goffman's foremost example of a nonperson in high society is the servant, a role which by its nature is often perceived as so irrelevant to important social interaction that for practical purposes the person simply isn't there. Confessions, tender secrets, and sensitive plans are routinely made in a "private" situation with servants remaining present. Goffman's definition of the term is interesting because it spotlights the importance of communication in determining and typing nonpersons. Nonpersons are those who are ". . . present during the interaction but in some respects do not take the role either of performer or audience, nor do they . . . pretend to be what they are not."[1]

I have sadly and reluctantly observed that students in American education are often seen as nonpersons by those in control of classrooms and institutions. Decisions are made, lectures given, tests evaluated, gossip exchanged, and all this in a climate of neglect for the individual personalities and response-abilities of what psychologist Kenneth Keniston calls "the faces in the lecture room."[2] I'll get more into such claims later, but for now let me refer you again to Goffman for his warning that such a situation can become dangerously reciprocal. "It would seem," he writes, "that the role of non-person usually carries with it some subordination and disrespect, but we must not underestimate the degree to which the person who is given or who takes such a role can use it as a defense. And it must be added that situations can arise when subordinates find that the only feasible way that they can handle a superordinate is to treat him as if he were not present."[3] Students who become victims of depersonalization may seek justification in depersonalizing teachers. Teachers, in noting callousness and lack of warmth in students, see little reason for person-centered relationships with students. Their communication behavior is reinforced. The cycle is fed.

A student once confided to me his feeling that cheating and lying to teachers was all right because teachers didn't care about him anyway, and because they consistently take unfair advantage of students. I asked him why he was telling me this; he responded that I was an "exception,"

---

[1] Erving Goffman, *The Presentation of Self in Everyday Life* (Garden City, N.Y.: Anchor Books, 1963), p. 151.

[2] Kenneth Keniston, "The Faces in the Lecture Room," in *The Contemporary University: U. S. A.*, ed. Robert S. Morison (Boston: Houghton Mifflin, 1966), pp. 315-349.

[3] Goffman, p. 152.

students as real people

that I could be trusted. That made me feel very warm—for a while, until I had a chance to think over the implications. Had he just flattered me with another lie, fully justified from his point of view? How can mutual trust hurdle such a barrier?

Trust cannot develop in the interaction of nonpersons. Formulas and rituals and the external mechanics of talking and hearing can develop, but not trust. Trust only comes as a result of a communicative relationship involving persons; that relationship becomes *personal,* and each participant becomes conscientiously real for the other(s).

So, now, you're beginning to understand the meanings I have for "person" (I hope). That doesn't mean you necessarily agree, either about the concept or about the state of our educational system. There are too many visions of the world for me to expect ours to be totally congruent. Besides, a friend once told me that if the two of us thought exactly alike, one of us would be superfluous.

The Concept of Person

I've tried to think through the idea of person by considering those I've known who were especially capable of maintaining communicative relationships. There are a number of things they seem to have in common: (1) they believe they are in control of themselves and thus are freely able to affect their environments in significant ways, (2) they are actively engaged in developing a unique and important idea of self-worth, (3) they seem to be more "whole" than many around them, recognizing the complementary natures of intellect and emotion, and (4) they seem to realize that living and loving and communication and (especially) persons are processes, not things. Please bear in mind that these criteria taken together construct only my concept of an "ideal type." Don't be discouraged or resentful if you don't know many of these people; I don't either. And don't feel frustrated and alone if the ideas don't describe you right now. I regret that I usually fall short of these criteria and am often confused by my environment; unable to reconcile my behavioral closedness with my philosophy, often unable to decide if I'm real or concocted. Suspecting the latter, I wonder how authors of most textbooks can be so *sure* about things. My students are sometimes surprised to encounter a teacher who admits to being confused, but I take a certain pride in it, actually. Confusion is a valuable indicator of future learning and areas of self-direction that is negated if you are fearful of what it does to you. Welcome confusion, I tell myself, and deal with it. The one thing that aids me most in dealing with my own confusion is the realization that although those around me may affect my environment, I am primarily in control of me. Therefore, I tend to stress the importance of the first of the four indicators of "person-ness."

are students persons?

Interior Regulation

Toward the end of a recent term, I was followed out of the class-room by two separate groups of three students anxious to discuss a grade I'd assigned to their group presentations in class. To be slightly more specific, they were questioning my judgment and fairness, and doing so with uncanny persistency for about forty-five minutes each. The second group politely waited off to the side while the first had their shots, and while I was grimly thinking that scouting reports should not be allowed. But they weren't bitching aimlessly; they all obviously felt something was amiss in our relationship and felt comfortable enough in the situation to discuss the matter openly. I tried to accept this as best I could, but felt myself becoming angrier by the minute, not so much that students would dare question my lofty proclamations but that they were evidently assuming (I perceived) that I somehow had a personal stake in giving the low grades, and that I perhaps even enjoyed doing it. Later, over warmed-over dinner, I'm afraid my wife heard more than she needed about how my students had made me mad and probably ruined my whole evening. I think I must have subjected her to approximately the same message I wished those six had remembered from an earlier class discussion. The problem of grading is perhaps my biggest frustra-tion in teaching, and though I feel manipulated by what sociologists call "institutional press" to engage in it, I dislike and fear grading time perhaps more than students. In the telling of the story, the same feelings bubbled and boiled, and, sure enough, my evening was ruined.

The point of such an extended example, which I only saw belat-edly, was that my anger was not forced on me at all by those people. *They* didn't make me mad, *they* didn't cause my down evening. When the subject of grading comes up, I am predisposed to anger. I look for it. It was *me* that made me angry and made me hard to live with for an evening. Spotlighting all the communication scapegoats in the world doesn't change the fact that each of us is primarily in control of what we do with our own emotions. Others don't hand you your feelings. You develop them as a result of your own need to perceive interpersonal reality in certain ways.

Effectively functioning persons seem to recognize the internal ori-gin of emotion and their ability to regulate effects of emotion on behav-ior. One worthwhile way to do this is by simple *telling*. Hugh Prather in *Notes to Myself* observed that feelings ". . . change simply by my becoming aware of them. When I acknowledge my feelings they become more positive. And they change when I express them. For example, if I tell a man I don't like him, I usually like him better."[4]

---

[4] Hugh Prather, *Notes to Myself* (Moab, Utah: Real People Press, 1970).

9

students as real people

Another of Prather's insights seems appropriate here as a qualification. I don't mean to imply that effectively functioning persons control what emotions they feel. Emotions arise as results of the most complicated and unpredictable of human activities—communication. They are not subject to prior censorship as are national security secrets about to be published. Prather writes: "Both my body and my emotions were given to me and it is as futile for me to condemn myself for feeling scared, insecure, selfish or revengeful as it is for me to get mad at myself for the size of my feet. I am not responsible for my feelings, but for what I do with them."[5] *Notes to Myself* reveals its author as no cardboard cutout. Hugh Prather seems a person.

Identity

The more I am able to regulate the effect of my own emotions on myself, the more I am aware of the full impact of communication with others. And as I've grown to study the effects of communication more and more, I think there's been a growth in understanding of how my interactions with others have shaped my identity, a feeling (most of the time) of being uniquely worthwhile.

There is some personal encouragement in this observation, because the real persons I've known all seem to have positive identities; they seem to know who, what, where, and why they are, and how they got that way. In other words, they are good reporters of self, and they are so open to each new bit of "news" that life becomes manageable, and fun.

Maybe the most sensitive book I've read about identity and self processes is M. C. Richards' *Centering: In Pottery, Poetry, and the Person.*[6] The author's organizing analogy is a prerequisite for her craft, centered clay on the potter's wheel. And in her explanation of how this soft malleable clay gets centered on the turning wheel prior to the molding necessary to a finished product, it becomes clear that to her the clay is an extension of self and that through metaphor it represents a person constantly in contact and dialogue with molding his or her uniqueness. She brings the poet's craft with words to bear on the persistent philosophical problem of whether we are or can be in the final analysis in control of our lives. She convinces me that centered persons are in control.

Centering yourself is an act of affirmation, an act of trying, an act of faith in the self that you could become. But its essence cannot be monological. You do not discover your identity by sitting down alone

---

[5] Ibid.

[6] M. C. Richards, *Centering: In Pottery, Poetry, and the Person* (Middletown, Conn.: Wesleyan University Press, 1962).

10

are students persons?

and passively thinking the matter through, giving miniature orations to yourself (I know; I've tried). You discover your self in dialogue, by listening to yourself talk and by noticing the effects of your talk both in the internal you and the external environment.[7] The development of self is a creative, artistic act, but one which does not really end in a finished object, like a pot. The interaction between the you that is and the you that will be is not susceptible to stop-action analysis or instant replay. Every move is accounted for in the you of the future. What you are now is an accumulating autobiography of your unique past.

The effectively functioning person recognizes more about himself or herself than uniqueness and change. Noticed also is the fact that a person is individualized, not an individualist. The process of maturation doesn't make people less unique; instead, individualization is increased as one's unique encounters multiply. But do we at the same time become more individualistic? Anthropoligist Ashley Montagu doesn't think so:

> It is one of the greatest of errors to assume—for it is nothing more than an erroneous assumption—that the older a person grows the more of an "individual" he grows to be. On the contrary, the older a person grows the more complex does the network of his social relationships become, and the more deeply involved does he become with society. In other words, he becomes less and less of an individual and more and more of a person.[8]

The same process of communication which makes divergent man's experiences makes convergent our needs to share those experiences.

While I've tended to discuss "self" and "identity" as singular terms, you've probably noticed that your social roles are so varied that you seem to be carrying around a basket-full of different "selves" to become as situations warrant. Transactional analysis spotlights three general "me's" depending upon my behavior—parent, adult, and child. I see so many more specific "me's" (in family, academic, serious, and frivolous contexts) that I sometimes lose track of my certainty that there is only one of me. A persistent topic among students in basic communication classes is whether people are being honest and "for real" if they are different in the presence of parents and peers, teachers and employers. Though you may suspect not, consider this approach. Your "self" cannot be one thing to others, but rather has to be a collective noun like "team," "group," or "clergy." I compare it to a sphere surrounded by those in my environment with whom I interact. No two observers of the sphere have exactly

---

[7] See George H. Mead, *Mind, Self, and Society* (Chicago: University of Chicago Press, 1934).

[8] Ashley Montagu, *The Humanization of Man* (New York: Grove Press Evergreen Black Cat Edition, 1964), p. 63.

11

students as real people

the same perspective on it, and therefore can't look upon the same me. There is inevitably some overlap, but each observer has available a unique view of a particular circle; my self is thus inevitably demonstrated differently in each different interaction and I needn't feel guilty about it. Whether fortunately or unfortunately, in fact, I have become pretty adept at rotating the "self sphere" so as to allow others a look at only the part of me I wish to divulge.

In sum, the effectively functioning person is engaged in developing a unique, ever-changing identity. Such a sense of self acts as what behaviorists sometimes call a psychological anchor—a reference point from which individual decisions can be based and new information assimilated. Without identity, organisms cannot develop meaning from their lives or help supply meaning for the lives of others. Systems of positive identity facilitate community.

Wholeness

I'm not sure there is such a thing as a fact divorced from emotion, or a cognition unattended by affect. "November 22, 1963" is about as factual as I can get in a statement. But if you have any degree of understanding for why I chose this particular date* for an example, you must have an emotion attached to it. Similarly, describe the appearance of your body—factual information—and see if you can hold back strong feelings of satisfaction and/or dissatisfaction, relief and/or shame, pleasure and/or pain.

Despite this, however, many seem to have worked hard to suppress one aspect or the other from their conscious processes, to approach thinking and interacting and being as much as possible from only a rational, fact-oriented level, or only an emotional and often intuitive level. My own experience is my best example here. I remember being rewarded at a fairly early age by my parents for an ability to relate to adults in their own language. This ability in effect meant I had learned to go out of my way to deny some impulsive but pleasant emotions because they were childish, and substitute a more adult fact-centered personal rhetoric. The pride of my mother and father was apparent, as was the pride of a number of teachers in my tendencies to abstract, to intellectualize, to analyze, to toy with concepts. All my reinforcements pointed in the same direction. I don't remember doubting that my behavior was what school should be all about.

School to me was a place where teachers were to be emulated, and teachers were concerned with "covering ground" which was strewn with "information" which could be "recalled." Magic words from my past. My

---

*John F. Kennedy was assassinated on that day.

are students persons?

present is different, though I cannot pinpoint what changed me. Somewhere along the way there were experiences which altered the internal momentum, telling me I was becoming one of the more knowledgeable partial persons on my block. I now relate to David Nyberg's experience with several school administrators and planners. In charge of a small group communication experience designed for such personnel, he decreed that their talk could only relate to those physically present in the room, and could not refer to past or future events. He found they were unable and unwilling to conform; the language of the present was beyond their reach. Frustration and hostility followed, because:

> The language they couldn't use, the language about the present, is a "whole person" language which is basically a feeling language. A person always has a feeling at a given time; he may not have a cogent thought to go with it, but he always has a feeling. When he is able to recognize the feeling, accept it, and express it in words or movement, then thoughts and feelings merge. Thoughts alone make a "head" language which comes on cold (mistakenly termed "objective" by its protectors) and often domineering or pompous. Men like the planners use a "head" language in their work most of the time, and they use it (because they are "professionals" after all) when confronting the community. They know it separates them from the community and exemplifies their status, and that's why they use it.[9]

Nyberg hits me between the eyes. The more head language I used to satisfy teachers who used head language, the more estranged I became from the emotions I needed to make myself more whole, more stable, and more versatile as a communicator. I became estranged from what was necessary to understand others, and myself.

Process-orientation

Events happen. Processes are happening. Objects are. Processes are becoming. The chief differences semantically relate to motion and change. Processes are like events but in motion, like objects but in transition. What we call events are time-specific; you can define their duration by starting and stopping points. "It's not here yet. Here it comes. Now it's started. Here it is. There it goes. There it was." What we call objects are space-specific; you can define their size by boundaries. "It's in this place. It's not in that place." Conceptually, however, processes are in many ways neither time-specific nor space-specific.

---

[9] David Nyberg, *Tough and Tender Learning* (Palo Alto, California: National Press Books, 1971), p. 91.

students as real people

It is easier for me to understand processes as being closer in meaning to events than to objects. Typical dictionary definitions refer to process in chronological ways: "the course of being done," "continuing development," etc. But I'm more concerned that you see that *you* (normally an object, perhaps, in your language) are actually a process. Real persons have realized the implications of this.

Psychologist Carl Rogers noted several trends in his clients over a period of time. One of the most important was that ". . . the individual moves toward more acceptantly being a process, a fluidity, a changing."[10] By this I believe he means that such individuals began to see that each experience sets stages for succeeding ones, subtly altering the ground rules for the predictability game. They began to see that change is the norm in human communication, that personal stability comes not in arresting change, but in accepting it, in using it as insight into personal uniqueness.

The vessel that is the centered you (to retain M. C. Richards' metaphor) is always emerging in different ways from the molding and shaping of your own experience. This is the difference between being static product and becoming dynamic flux, a distinction important to Buckminster Fuller:

> I live on Earth at present,
> and I don't know what I am.
> I know that I am not a category.
> I am not a thing—a noun.
> I seem to be a verb,
> an evolutionary process—
> an integral function of the universe.[11]

American Education and Its Expectations of Students

At the beginning of this chapter I implied that students are too often perceived by teachers and schools as not having person-potential. If you were perceived as having such potential, your educational experiences would have been geared to helping you develop your own (literally) *personal* style which would have freed you in significant ways. My idea is that school would have stressed your abilities as an interior regulator, would have encouraged your uniqueness as developed through

---

[10] Carl R. Rogers, "Toward Becoming a Fully Functioning Person," in *Perceiving, Behaving, Becoming* (Washington, D. C.: Association for Supervision and Curriculum Development, 1962), p. 25.

[11] From *I Seem To Be a Verb* by R. Buckminster Fuller, with Jerome Agel and Quentin Fiore; copyright © 1970 by Bantam Books, Inc. By permission of the publisher.

are students persons?

extensive interaction with others, would have emphasized your need to cope with emotional as well as informational matters, would have convinced you that being in process and caught up in intense personal changes are okay.

I hope your education helped you in those ways. I was too busy memorizing the Civil War.

The Impact of Expectation

One of the central concerns of human communication research has been to study the impact of interpersonal expectation. Much of the literature on perception indicates that we often hear and see what we expect to hear and see; "response sets" are formed by behaving in accordance with personal expectations. Studies of small group contexts show perceived expectations of others as primary stimulants to conformity. Research in voting behavior, subcultures, and reference groups shows our attitudes and actions are routinely weighed against expectations of relevant groups.

Expectation can have positive or negative effects. Robert Rosenthal's "Pygmalion Effect" is a startling example of both.[12] You've probably heard people joke about "self-fulfilling prophecies," projected events that have come true seemingly because they've been talked about and are expected to come true. Rosenthal found that regardless of actual measured abilities of children, teachers who are told the children in their classes are bright find those students being more successful in school than students of teachers who erroneously believe their students are below average in intelligence. Simply, students who are expected by their teachers to do well do so, and students who are not expected to do well fulfill *that* expectation. Rosenthal developed a four-point explanation for the success of the high expectation students: their teachers provided (1) a supportive and emotionally warm climate, (2) specific and active feedback, (3) more effort, and (4) more encouragement of student responsiveness.

The implications for teacher-student interaction are incredible! If I sincerely expect you to learn from this book and respect your ability to do so, that will show up as a kind of submessage you'll read and receive just as clearly as the words themselves. The result means increased chances that you'll learn something from it. But if I expect you to give the book a pitch, or "creatively ignore" it (as I've done with some of mine), you'll perceive that, too, *and it will affect your attitude negatively.*

Here's a really scary part of the problem. Educational critics Neil Postman and Charles Weingartner write that ". . . the critical content of

---

[12] See his description of relevant research in "The Pygmalion Effect Lives," *Psychology Today*, Sept. 1973, pp. 56-63.

students as real people

any learning experience is the method or process through which the learning occurs."[13] As a student, you learn to be a student better and sooner than you learn anything else—History, English, Philosophy, whatever. And any student worth his or her salt knows that one of the cardinal rules of studentness is being able to "read" and produce what a teacher wants. You've taught yourself to do that; it's in your survival manual.

This all adds up to one thing—if those who run schools expected students to be persons, they would be. But look around. Look within.

Perhaps different expectations are being fulfilled.

Behavioral Expectations of Students

At the base of it all, I'm excited and optimistic about current trends in education and in society, too, for that matter. Many dedicated, concerned people are working hard to effect changes which, though long due, are really inevitable. Schools will be humanized, and probably even as I write in this section about negative expectations and damaging effects, decisions are being made somewhere which will make schools more humane and warm places to be.

But I can't help but be a little worried as long as a thirteen-year-old can write, "When I first get up in the morning I feel fresh and it seems like it would be a good day to me. But after I get in school, things change and they seem to turn into problems for me. And by the end of the day I don't even feel like I'm young. I feel tired."[14] Chances are slim such a student will seek out "higher" education with any depth of commitment.

In this section I'll try to describe what I see as the major school expectations which operate to depersonalize, delearn, and restrain students on all levels. Many of the expectations in some form or another are justified by educators in statements similar to: "This is the way life is, tough and unrelenting. Students are better for having been exposed to the discipline of dealing with such problems in schools." True, if you think of school as shackle practice for the dungeon of the rest of your life. False, if you think of a school as a place where you could joyfully and responsibly learn how to make the rest of your life a continuing education.

The prime organizing expectation imposed upon American students is that they will be passively obedient. The teacher determines what will go on in the class; students often are present merely as respon-

---

[13] Neil Postman and Charles Weingartner, *Teaching as a Subversive Activity* (New York: Delta Books, 1969), p. 19.

[14] Stephen M. Joseph, ed., *The Me Nobody Knows* (New York: Avon Discus Edition, 1969), p. 20. "Victor Y" is the author.

are students persons?

dents. Even their responses must be bounded carefully, as students should not influence decisions too often if the teacher-centered model of instruction is to be retained. Our society has somehow injected the schools with the assumption that unattended students are highly prone to disorganization and destructiveness. Therefore, they most need to be subjected to what Paul Goodman calls "animal restraint."[15] Many commentators on education marvel at the lack of trust exhibited by teachers in classrooms. "Order" is so often the most serious criterion that Peter Marin's perspective both amuses and frightens me:

> From first to twelfth grade we acclimatize students to a fundamental deadness and teach them to restrain themselves for the sake of "order."

I remember a talk I had with a college student.

> "You know what I love to do," he said. "I love to go into the woods and run among the trees."
> "Very nice," I said.
> "But it worries me. We shouldn't do it."
> "Why not?" I asked.
> "Because we get excited. It isn't *orderly.*"
> "Not orderly?"
> "Not orderly."
> "Do you run into the trees?"
> "Of course not."
> "Then it's orderly," I said.[16]

Such a student seems unfree. He's renounced his capacity of interior regulation. He's placed obedience to institutional desires superior to recognizing and acting on his own feelings. He's been taught by expectation that his feelings are apart from, and not a part of, the needs and goals of schools.

Thus begins a cycle of negativity. Once a student quits expecting that his or her emotions will be important in education, it's only a brief step to teachers and administrators routinely neglecting interpersonal emotional needs of students. Students when assumed emotionless react in futility, sharing few strong emotions with teachers, which in turn frustrates teachers hoping to "get a rise" out of listless listeners with a carefully conceived lesson plan.

---

[15] Paul Goodman, *Compulsory Mis-education and The Community of Scholars* (New York: Vintage Books, 1962), p. 27.
[16] Peter Marin, "The Open Truth and Fiery Vehemence of Youth: A Sort of Soliloquy," *The Center Magazine,* January 1969, p. 68.

students as real people

The school's view of young humans as disorganized and destructive has set into operation a chain of assumptions which makes students untenable partners in the building of their own educations. The sad irony is that the idea couldn't be more inaccurate. Ashley Montagu orients us more sensibly. "There is widespread belief," he writes, "that a newborn baby is a rather selfish, disorganized, or unorganized, wild kind of creature. . . ." However, the child is actually "one of the most highly organized creatures on the face of the earth, and organized not for brattishness but for love."[17] If my classes seem disorganized and spiteful, should I be assuming that more discipline is required, more order, more emphasis on curtailing emotions? Or should I assume that most students have somehow been forced to exchange their innately positive orderliness in favor of an artificial and destructive brand which compels revolt?

Students are not only expected to be passively obedient and emotionless, but they are also expected to be wrong, the effects of which are every bit as predictable. Noel McInnis' hypothetical statement to a college freshman illustrates this clearly and succinctly: "Twelve years in a system of negative reinforcement has tended to make you a master of the art of feeling inferior."[18] Most grading procedures have focused on "mistakes," providing penalties for student learning attempts which didn't pan out immediately, or duplicate the teacher's preconceptions.

At the start of every quarter, I ask my students in "Oral Communication of Ideas," basically a freshman/sophomore course, to identify on paper what they feel to be their greatest strengths and most pressing weaknesses as communicators. Though no one ever seems to have any trouble on the latter, many are unable to think of any distinguishing positive feature which characterizes their approach to interpersonal relations. Usually it doesn't take long for me to spot strengths in these students that they are unable to perceive or unwilling to admit because of general and pervasive feelings of inferiority. Skepticism usually awaits my idea that every person in the class is already an expert on communication in a variety of styles and contexts, or else they wouldn't be able to

---

[17] Montagu, p. 100. Such misunderstanding certainly continues through college:

The tacit assumption made by the faculty and administration in organizing the college or university is that students are, by and large, simple-minded savages who will destroy the peace, order, and reputation of a school if they are not controlled and kept at bay. As a result, despite some external differences, the organizational structure of many modern higher educational institutions is not terribly different from that of penal institutions, with the single important exception that a student is relatively free to leave the college or university.

See The Committee on the Student in Higher Education, *The Student in Higher Education* (New Haven, Connecticut: The Committee on the Student in Higher Education, 1968), p. 39.

[18] Noel McInnis, quoted in Gail E. Myers and Michele Tolela Myers, *The Dynamics of Human Communication: A Laboratory Approach* (New York: McGraw-Hill, 1973), p. 107.

are students persons?

transact their daily formal and informal business. "Who's he trying to shuck?" say those who can't believe I'm serious. But I am. It just seems difficult for some students to deal with my assumption that they are already effective communicators who are simply in the class to sensitize themselves to new perspectives on relationships. They are not wrong or deficient as persons.

If persons develop an identity by listening to themselves talk and by listening to the reactions of others, the American student is clearly in trouble; most of those in charge of structuring their educational experiences expect them not to interact. When interaction is inevitable, it's effectively ignored by teachers, administrators, and researchers in frighteningly systematic ways. Scour the professional writing on educational methods if you have the time. You'll find precious little material relating to how students form subcultures, how students can be their own teachers, how they can cooperate in helping each other learn. It's almost all about how teachers can motivate students. The fourth expectation of students is that they will not participate in effective learning-oriented interaction with other students. Educators seem to assume learning is something someone does in isolation, that education is a "one-to-many" process, that students are "inoculated" with information and attitudes like the mass audience was assumed to be in earlier days of mass communication research. It wasn't true in general society and it's not true in the subsociety of schools. But the assumption of its truth toughens the already formidable barriers to communication among students and makes effective learning-oriented interaction take a back seat to "passing-the-time" interaction.

The final expectation flows naturally from the other four, namely, schools expect you to be impotent (academically). Not too many years ago, the academic world started to notice an essay written in anger by a college teacher in California, Jerry Farber.[19]

"The Student As Nigger" was intended to stimulate students to see how their seeming powerlessness in the educational system can be transformed into decision-making importance. The effectiveness of Farber's metaphor is evidenced in the current status of his book; it's already considered somewhat passé. Students have since begun to communicate more in meaningful university-wide committees, participating with faculty and administrators in important deliberations. But it's a rough transition for many who have been drilled from childhood into making *no* decisions about school policy, and an equally rough transition for many of their mentors who customarily deride student abilities. The residue of student and faculty cultures, once sifted through, amounts to a need for

---

[19] Found in Farber's subsequent book, *The Student As Nigger* (New York: Pocket Books, 1970).

students as real people

the ritualization of superior-subordinate relationships. Students too often not only accept this, but encourage it, even when working alongside faculty and administration. They seem distrustful of situations in which such ritual is not pushed upon them.

A vivid memory of mine concerns a ready-to-graduate senior, a bright, perceptive, devil's advocate type who had to be reconvinced almost daily that studying interpersonal communication was worthwhile. At the end of the quarter, I felt we had established a perhaps reluctant but nevertheless healthy respect for each other. But there still remained a lack of trust stemming from his perception that ours was hardly a "class" at all, compared to others he'd taken. Was I toying with the class? Was I serious that education could proceed in such an experiential, non-"content" way? His (very cordial and sincere) departing remarks: "Not bad, not bad. Were we some sort of experimental group? Is there a control group somewhere?" In an atmosphere where students generated initiative, responsibility, and decisions, he still couldn't believe that manipulation wasn't at the heart of the freedom. Students have been manipulated for too long.

As with a number of social problems, the source of student powerlessness is clearer than the implications. Melvin Seeman's fascinating essay in *Psychology Today* corroborates his description of a central idea in the Coleman Report on Equality of Educational Opportunity in the United States. "The dramatic finding," he states, "was that pupil achievement was more deeply affected by the pupil's sense of powerlessness . . . than by objective advantages such as the character of the library, teacher qualifications, and counseling services."[20] Hopefully, current trends of involvement in decision-making will mean a new sense of worth for students. Hopefully, you'll begin to notice that your opinions about education are being heard. Only then have we structured the kinds of expectations of your behavior which open learning contexts, and encourage reciprocal open expectations from you.

Why This Book Is about Interpersonal Communication

I hope you're starting to identify with my emphasis on the concept of "person" as the central orientation of an overall message. For it is only when we sense our own possibilities and are treated as persons that we can hope for satisfying relationships. From an individual's point of view, all of communication can be subdivided into just two factors—*giving opportunities* and *taking others into account*. It is clear to me that I was not often given full opportunity to learn in schools, nor did others take my

---

[20] Melvin Seeman, "Alienation: A Map," *Psychology Today*, August 1971, p. 95.

are students persons?

responses (bad or good) much into account. But my behavior was frighteningly similar. I denied teachers opportunities to explain and avoided taking them into account as individual persons. In many ways I'm sure I objectified them—made them nonpersons—more than they did me.

I've become so convinced that education is not usually viewed as communication that I want to devote the next chapter to that topic. The "handle," though, for analyzing communication in schools is inherent in *this* chapter. Inter*person*al communication.

In the everyday usage of "person," I guess most of what we call human communication is interpersonal by definition; it happens as a result of the interaction of men and women. Such communication is inevitable and natural if we're to function socially. But what I'm talking about as interpersonal communication is far from inevitable and natural. My perspective on the person leads me to believe that interpersonal communication has to do with *personal* matters (interior regulation, identity, wholeness, process) and with *personal* assumptions of interdependence by each participant. Here is the focus of all satisfying learning. Give an opportunity. And take the other into account as a person.

Such actions seem all too rare in American education. The intent of this chapter has been to establish several perspectives: a definition of person appropriate to the study of communication, an elaboration of how effectively functioning persons view themselves and are viewed by others, a demonstration of how the expectations of schools in many ways subvert the development of persons, and a rationale out of all this for studying interpersonal communication.

3

education
as
communication

My oldest son taught me something very important one morning when he was three years old. While eating breakfast from our respective bowls of cereal, Eric began a game of giving me some of his in return for some of mine (which was identical to his, physically if not psychologically). He wasn't trading exactly; he just enjoyed the process of giving and getting, interaction for its own joyful sake. His word for it was "sharing." *We* were sharing, he emphasized in his uncontrollable penchant for labeling everything. And he was participating in sharing even when he was receiving the cereal.

Aside from making me feel good to recall the story, my major purpose here is to confess how diminished my concept of sharing had become. Sharing, before Eric's insight hit me, had become in my mind a behavior that one person did by giving objects to another whether the desire to give was there or not. I've concluded that most adults (if they use the word at all) have this one-way conception of sharing: I share by giving to you an object which used to be mine. But Eric encouraged me to see the idea in a new and exciting way; a way analogous to the concept of communication I'd like to stress later. In Eric's theory, we share whether we're giving or getting if we have defined something as common between us, from which we both are able to benefit.

Sharing is a "we-process." It is not an "I-process" like contributing to a charity, driving to school, or carrying books.

Communication is also a "we-process." I don't communicate. I talk and I act; I form messages. Talk and action emanate from me. Communication doesn't. Communication is a word describing what goes on between me and someone else when we are together in a relationship, sharing something. The something we are sharing may be important or trivial, exciting or dull, conscious or unconscious. But all of our behavior

22

education as communication

in sharing contributes to evoking some kind of meaning, and thus changes us in some way—and for this reason is important.

I can be said to communicate only in the limited and inaccurate sense that I sometimes colloquially say I've played a basketball game. You know I'm not able to comprise the whole game by myself; I only contribute to the playing of the game by my actions and my talk. The ultimate development and resolution of the game depends upon the interaction of my actions and words with those of others. (For the curious—my contributions don't seem to be decisive, since in two league last winter, teams on which I played won a total of one game!)

I talk a lot. But that doesn't mean I communicate well. That's not for me to determine, but for us to determine. I don't comprise the whole game. If you say "I communicate," maybe others will understand your verbal shorthand which was intended to mean that you have only contributed to communication. But maybe they won't, and it's still a good distinction to keep in mind, if only for your confrontations with people who seem to believe unswervingly that what they say has inherent meaning and that you are not at all an important part of an interaction. Keeping in mind the distinction, as a matter of fact, has occasionally kept me from being one of those people.

The main thought in this chapter is that the communication process and the educational process, in their narrow as well as broad senses, should be considered in precisely the same ways.

Considering Interpersonal Communication

My most urgent desires in college as a speech major were to give a better speech, tighten up that organization, become more fluent, win more arguments, and analyze or intellectualize more political rhetoric than anyone else in town. I succeeded some and failed some, but by and large gave it the good ole college try.

I came late to the realization that while preparing speeches is important in many situations, I was basically teaching myself to be a performer. And as a performer I was always a little off balance and ill-at-ease even when being "rewarded." So when some colleagues became interested in studying informal communication relationships, they easily caught my ear. I listened carefully. A lot of us listened. Lately, in fact, infatuation with writing about the quality of relationships has reached fad proportions both in academic and popular cultures.[1]

---

[1] Your local bookstore probably stocks more "self-help" books than you could comfortably carry away which purport to help you better your interpersonal relationships. Many are best-sellers.

students as real people

The study of humanistic interpersonal communication is so attractive to me because it stresses nonperformance. It takes the pressure off and makes my me the public me. It takes communication into the real world of the relationships I live with daily and seems to suggest new ways to cope with them. To the extent I choose to "perform" in these situations, I may expect others to distrust me because I've cut myself off from them. Performance encourages an audience to wonder what the reality behind it is like; are you one of the millions who have wondered what Johnny Carson is *really* like? But to the extent I permit myself to invite dialogue, I may expect others to welcome, and perhaps, embrace me.

Interpersonal communication exhibits several interlocking natures. It is dialogue, it is process, it is perception, it is symbol, it is nonverbal, it is above all *relationship.*

The Dialogical Nature of Communication

Some of my instructors stressed to me the importance of the "delivery" of speeches. I remember thinking at the time that that was a strange word; now it seems positively subversive. In communication nothing is "delivered" in the same sense that our postman delivers the letter you write me, as I'll receive exactly the same sheet of paper you sent. Ideas certainly are not "delivered" or "transmitted" in interpersonal situations simply because each of us is unique. The meaning of my world is only inside me and cannot be packaged neatly and delivered to another person.

The most important insight about communication is at the same time one of the silliest sounding statements conceivable. I hesitate to write it for fear you'll chuckle, but it's late at night and I feel untense and willing to try.

I am not you and you are not me.

That's it. But please consider its implications and the times when our assumptions deny it. If I, in monologue, perform for you a joke, "delivering" it with all the skill I can muster, and you don't laugh, a very curious thing often happens. I blame *you!* I assume that because the joke is funny to me that it is inherently funny and therefore should be funny to you. I assume, in effect, that you are me, at least as far as that one message is concerned.

A condition of dialogue assumes that each of us has a uniqueness which is of value, and that we both need to participate in order to develop a common meaning for the messages which characterize our relationship. In monologue, I only know if the joke is funny *to me,* and you only know if the joke is funny *to you.* In dialogue, we verbally compare notes to find if our unique and individually created meanings can come together to mean the joke is funny *for us.* In dialogue, we are not

education as communication

immediately tempted to blame the other person if communication is not all it could be. The concept of no-fault auto insurance seems worthwhile; so does the concept of no-fault communication. In dialogue, each accepts responsibility for the development of common meaning, but it does not help us to assign blame or find fault. No-fault insurance says, "an accident has happened; let's cut the red tape of blame and deal with fixing the cars." No-fault communication says, "we've hit a snag in understanding each other; let's cut the red tape of blame and deal with fixing the relationship."

Students are sometimes surprised to find how inaccurate human understanding can be when participating in "rumor," a simple birthday party-like game we sometimes do in class. A person who hears a relatively simple one paragraph news story once in a no-feedback environment is expected to explain its essence to the next student, who did not hear the orginal story. That student then describes it to a new volunteer who hasn't heard either the original or the first interpretation, and so on until five students have heard the story in turn. The exercise usually produces a story from number five which bears zero resemblance to the original, much to the pious delight of onlookers (including me) who aren't at all sure that they could do better. The value of feedback and therefore the power of dialogue has been robbed from the volunteers. A second trial with feedback inserted at each link of the chain usually produces enough improvement in accuracy to convince us that effective communication is indeed a two-way responsibility.

But how often do we in our classroom behavior come close to duplicating the *first* trial? Consider yourself in a lecture hall sitting on a question you're too embarrassed to ask. You've set up for yourself a no-feedback environment just as destructive as the contrived rules to the rumor game. You sit in safe but unproductive isolation instead of inviting the professor out of monologue into a more mutually satisfying conversation. Or consider me, or someone like me, up front in that hall assuming (hoping?) that the lack of questions indicates your acceptance and understanding of my ideas. There is safety there, too, but the lack of dialogue is ultimately as unproductive for me as for you, since I lose a chance to learn of your learning.

The process of dialogue will foster growth only when we assume together that our messages have *not* been interpreted as we meant them to be. Then we are energized to seek together a resolution of meanings which satisfies us both. The absence of this mutual seeking in education disqualifies it as education. "If teaching occurs only when learning does," writes Raymond H. Reno, "then education is a mutual enterprise which is possible only under the conditions of dialogue."[2]

---

[2] Raymond H. Reno, *The Impact Teacher* (St. Paul: 3M Education Press, 1967), p. 133.

students as real people

The Process Nature of Communication

To say that communication is a process implies two other statements. First, it implies that communication and movement (motion) are intimately related. Psychic motion occurs always—thought, images, attitudes, meanings. And all this motion results from the impact of preceding messages. People are changed, become psychologically in motion, by anything you say, and for that matter, anything they say. Not only must you assume that "I am not you and you are not me," you must assume that "I am not the I I used to be, even a second ago." Each single perception alters the perceptual system. Perhaps the effect is slight, but it's still present and perhaps more important because of the cumulative slightness of the change.

I sometimes forget that communication is this dynamic, that it's actually a process instead of a *thing* (which I can analyze while holding it still, perhaps under my rational microscope) or an *event* (which I could record in linear sequence for later analysis, complete with definite starting and stopping points). Both things and events "hold still" better than processes and are relatively easy to talk about because of that simplification. Calling communication a thing or an event, though, is an oversimplification. As I've mentioned in a previous chapter, things could be termed space-specific, in that you can tell where they start and where they end. Events are time-specific, in that you can tell when they start and when they end. Processes blur all the distinctions; they are bounded neither spatially nor chronologically. They exist in continuous flow, continuous motion, continuous adjustment.

An apple is a thing. An apple being picked is an event. Growth is a process which interrelates with, affects, and in many ways determines the nature of the apple and the picking of it.

I've just reread the last couple of paragraphs, and they sound stuffy. But I want to leave them pretty much as they are because I worked so hard on the wording. Instead of changing them, let me add something which may make both my view of communication and me seem more tangible to you. I wrote it not long ago in connection with something unrelated to this book, and make no claim for it except that it expresses with some economy of language the relationships among being in process, being frustrated, and being.

The basis of life . . .
The basis of life
(How pretentious!)
And the basis of strife

education as communication

Are the same?
How?
Are the same.
Change.
Tough to accept
Impossible to change
Change.

Why do I struggle to assume
My today-me
And
My yesterday-me
My now-me
And
My minute-ago me
Are the same?

Life basis and strife basis
May be the same:
Change.

But me
And ...
And ...
And ...
Me
Can't be
The same.

Intervals and recognitions and awarenesses
Change me.

But most of all,
Tough but possible
To accept,

I change me.

The second implication of labeling communication a process is its
inevitability. Communication doesn't go away when we are neglecting it,
it just deteriorates in quality. If you and I are both cognizant of our
relationship, then we don't have the choice of whether to communicate.

students as real people

We only have the choice of how to communicate. Because communication is a process, it is inevitable.

A smart-alecky mood once stimulated me to ask a class, "If I wanted to stop communicating with you right now, what could I do?" "Quit talking," came a voice from my left, and though I thought I detected an extra ring of sincerity, I did so. My facial features quickly formed an involuntary message, though, and some of my meaning became shared meaning. "Turn your back on us." Okay, here goes. But my prolonged silence was interpreted as another message, and a little more of my meaning for my actions became clear. "Leave." Wow! This was getting to be fun. And out I went. I think I slammed the door, which wasn't playing fair, but you've got to succumb to an impulse or two now and then. After waiting in the hall a respectable period of time, I re-entered to a discussion of how no matter what I did or what they did to "cut off" communication, the process persisted. The human organism in relationship is a meaning-generator. We all try to make sense out of our environments by noting and developing interpretations of others' actions. And when we realize that silence and absence are among the most potent of human messages, the inevitability of communication becomes clearer to us.

The Perceptual Nature of Communication

Each of us sees the world in a way duplicated by no one else. This can be said with assurance because no one else can duplicate our experiences . . . which make our memories different . . . which make our preferences different . . . which support our differing value and identity systems . . . out of which come a variety of attitudes which predispose us to see the world in internally consistent and/or self-satisfying ways.

Kenneth Boulding's *The Image* contains a clear description of how each person develops a unique style of perceiving the world ("the image") which determines and in many ways is determined by how he or she transacts with the world. But behavior at any one point in time "depends on the image."[3] And the meaning we develop in response to incoming messages is determined by the effects they produce in our images.

If it is true that a central concept of communication is that "I am not you and you are not me," with its corollary, "I can't be you and you can't be me," then the perceptual factors in communication become crucial. When we're together, I can't work with your perception of you. I have no access to it; it's within you. I have to build my own perception of

---

[3] Kenneth E. Boulding, *The Image: Knowledge in Life and Society* (Ann Arbor: University of Michigan Press, 1961), p. 6.

28

education as communication

you and react to that, letting my behavior flow from my own image. When we talk, my you and your you, my me and your me all interact:

> My field of experience is . . . filled not only by my direct view of myself (ego) and of the other (alter), but of what we shall call *meta*perspectives—*my view* of the *other's* (your, his, her, their) *view* of me. I may not actually be able to see myself as others see me, but I am constantly supposing them to be seeing me in particular ways, and I am constantly acting in the light of the actual or supposed attitudes, opinions, needs, and so on the other has in respect of me.

> From this we see that as my identity is refracted through the media of the different inflections of "the other"—singular and plural, male and female, you, he, she, them—so my identity undergoes myriad metamorphoses or *alter*ations, in terms of the others I become to the others.[4]

I am different in different relationships not only because of how I act, but because of how the other perceives me. The word "transaction" is a good way to describe this situation of communication in which we each help to define the other, constructing the image of the other to which we speak while we disclose the nature of that image.

This view of the perceptual nature of communication, while possibly frustrating in that my understanding of you can never be complete, presents immense possibilities for humanizing relationships. If we are to communicate, we need to team up.

> Today I saw a part of you which was possible only because of my presence
> And I was changed
> Not only because of the new perception
> But because I discovered I could help it along

> So
> I saw a part of me which was possible only because of your presence
> And you were changed
> Not only because of my change
> But because you discovered you could help me along
> Just by you being not-me

> We cooperated in possibility and discovery and change
> We're a team.

---

[4] R. D. Laing, H. Phillipson, and A. R. Lee, *Interpersonal Perception: A Theory and A Method of Research* (N. Y.: Springer, 1966), p. 4.

students as real people

The Symbolic Nature of Communication

We use words to help us carry our physical and historical environments around with us. With words, we can recall mutually a pond and re-experience its beauty together without going back to the woods. We can recall a friend mutually and re-experience his effect on our relationship together without his physical presence. We can share with each other our separate but interlocking perceptions of the beauty of a painting.

But the word "painting" is not a painting, "him" is not *him,* and saying "pond" doesn't reproduce one. Words stand for reality. They are substitutes—symbols. We've divided up reality into categories and agreed upon labels to be assigned to each category. And just as reality has only the meaning we assign to it, so does the label mean only what we want it to. Words are social inventions, tools to help us establish connection, giving me increased access to you and your world.

If enough of us notice we're using the same word in pretty much the same way, that tool will become more or less institutionalized and will appear in a dictionary complete with an "established" meaning. This, of course, doesn't imply the word means exactly that to any one person. Instead, the dictionary acts as a kind of overgeneralized public opinion poll on the use of language within a social group. Words mean what we agree for them to mean.

Thus it follows that words don't carry meaning to me. They may come to me from the outside, but I am in charge of attributing meaning to them. How I do so often determines the nature of my relationships, and therefore, the nature of my learning.

The Nonverbal Nature of Communication

Think back on what you have studied throughout your education. The three "R's." Historical interpretations. Poetry. Chemistry from thick textbooks. Lectures, lectures, lectures.

Words.

Almost every minute of your education has been geared to improve or depend upon the quality of your understanding of language. Verbal communication—the communication which occurs as a result of the written and spoken word—is an extremely important facet of your education. Through it you gain access to a world you may not have known before and through it you increase your own abilities to widen that access.

Because of this importance and because of the educational system's emphasis on verbalizing, you may be lulled into thinking there is only

education as communication

one system of messages to be contended with in a conversation. "He has a message for me; I'd better try to figure out what it is," I sometimes think. But studying the nonverbal aspects of communication suggests another conclusion. He has a *variety* of messages for me. Some spoken, some unspoken. Some intentional, some unintentional. Some vocal, some visual. Consider the following scenario; it may remind you of an experience.

This guy has cheated you out of a grade for the last time. Here you are walking down the hall to his office and thinking "I'll never have the nerve to do it—to confront him." Maybe you won't when you get there. Uh-oh. The door is closed. That must mean he isn't there, you think and hope. But he's supposed to be. It's his office hour.

You tap your best "I hope he's not here" knock on the door while straightening the collar on the sport shirt you strategically decided to wear instead of the t-shirt the class saw you in all semester. "Come in." Unusually gruff, even for Johnson. You do, brushing the doorknob with your books, almost dropping them in a stupid betrayal of nervousness. "Dr. Johnson, I . . ." you begin in an unnaturally high pitch which makes you sound more like "Leave It To Beaver" Cleaver than a mature adult college student.

But you notice too late that Johnson is on the phone. He'd been looking down at the desk. Looking up only long enough to acknowledge yet another intrusion, he points to a chair on the opposite side of his desk and returns to his busy-bemused expression. "God, he's busy and irritated. I'm done for." But at least you now have a chance to catch your breath. Sitting there, you look around the room as your thumping heart begins to dethump a little.

Johnson is swiveling in his chair while you fidget in your stationary straightback chair. The expanse of his desk acts as a barrier, widening the gulf between him and you. You are cut off from him both emotionally and physically. The plaster, a dull gray, begins to stifle you: "I could never be creative here. The walls are closing in." Two whole walls are lined with books—the accumulated wisdom of centuries of historians. The books suddenly symbolize your ignorance *versus* Johnson's academic qualifications. *Three* diplomas, the only decorations, on the wall by the door. "Harvard, for God's sake." You suddenly feel very small. There's the stack of term papers. "If he hated my midterm, he'll despise the term paper."

The phone conversation is winding down and Johnson is preparing to hang up. Your heart begins to thump anew. Click. "Dr. Johnson, I . . ., uh . . ." Johnson has said nothing, but you know by

31

students as real people

his expression he's not hearing you. He motions "wait" with his right index finger and begins to write a note on his personalized memo pad. You shrink again. You're foiled again. Waiting and more waiting.

He looks up, remembering to smile as he glances at his watch. "Oh, hi," he states, "glad to see you."

Sure.

"What's on your mind—?" Doesn't remember your name.

Pause. Silence. Lump in throat. Noticeable.

"Well, Dr. Johnson," you start shakily, "I was wondering . . . if I could borrow that Schlesinger book you mentioned Tuesday. The library copy's been stolen."

Johnson has negated you and your real concerns long before a question was ever ventured. But he's said no in a very sneaky way. He's said it nonverbally. You've let yourself be intimidated by a potent system of nonverbal messages which he uses to define his role and your role, his personality and your personality, his importance and your importance. Yet if asked, he could deny every message. Maybe he's not even aware of them all.

Yet, believe it or not, there are still some students who either ignore or deny the importance of nonverbal communication. Randall Harrison reports that ". . . it has been estimated that in face-to-face communication not more than 35 percent of the social meaning is carried in the verbal messages,"[5] and although I'm not sure how to arrive at such a statistic, it's not difficult to see why this could be true. Consider the range of nonverbal messages displayed in the scenario I just described: silence, gestures, unintentional body movement, eye contact and facial expression, touching behavior, vocal cues (inflection, rate, volume, etc.), object display, appearance and dress, spatial relationships, manipulation of time, affective potential of color, and involuntary physiological factors.

Dr. Johnson's verbal message ("glad to see you") was contradicted by his nonverbal message (roughly, "you're pretty insignificant around here compared to me"). In such instances, which do you tend to believe? I'd wager you'd believe the nonverbal sooner since in general and at some level of your consciousness, you're aware that nonverbal communication reveals the true feelings of people sooner and that it is basically harder for people to control or fake. Of course, we need to attach significant qualifications to the interpretation of nonverbal cues—they are of-

---

[5] Randall Harrison, "Nonverbal Communication: Explorations into Time, Space, Action, and Object," in *Dimensions in Communication: Readings*, James H. Campbell and Hal W. Hepler, eds. (Belmont, California: Wadsworth, 1965), p. 161.

32

education as communication

ten more ambiguous than words and must be interpreted in context. Maybe we'd better not assume for sure that Dr. Johnson felt you were insignificant; maybe we should give him the benefit of our doubt. He may have been highly disturbed by a personal problem. His office style may have been determined by departmental policy, by the professor sharing it, or by mere convenience.

Your relationship with Johnson, though, was clearly more affected and defined by nonverbal factors than by verbal ones. This is true with all your relationships. Words are heard and understood only against a backdrop of simultaneous nonverbal cues. You will never completely trust Johnson until his nonverbal and verbal statements merge into a single coherent and consistent set of messages.

Communication as Relationship

You and I don't profitably study communication only by studying individuals. Focusing on the individual and his or her attitudes or statements distorts our perception of how interpersonal communication happens. Instead, a focus on relationships—what happens between two or more people who are aware of each others' presence—clarifies matters. Watzlawick, Beavin, and Jackson put it clearly:

> Every child learns at school that movement is something relative, which can only be perceived in relation to a point of reference. What is not realized by everyone is that this same principle holds for virtually every perception and, therefore, for man's experience of reality. Sensory and brain research have proved conclusively that only relationships can be perceived, and these are the essence of experience.[6]

But even though I've read this, I often find myself thinking that if I just understand the other person well enough—my wife, a student, my chairman, etc.—then I'll be able to decide how to improve "my communication" with him or her. This is impossible. Literally, I can't perceive the other person. What I'm perceiving is my relationship to the other, constantly in flux. It's not "my" communication, it's *ours*, and it's a function of our relationship. Paul Tournier writes of "all these people who come to see me," who ". . . take so much trouble over their efforts to describe themselves to me with strict accuracy; inevitably I form an image of them which derives as much from myself as from them."[7]

---

[6] Paul Watzlawick, Janet Helmick Beavin, and Don D. Jackson, *Pragmatics of Human Communication: A Study of Interactional Patterns, Pathologies, and Paradoxes* (N. Y.: W. W. Norton, 1967), p. 27.

[7] Paul Tournier, *The Meaning of Persons* (N. Y.: Harper and Row, 1957), p. 14.

students as real people

I don't interpret this idea as cynicism or an indication of the impossibility of effective or satisfying communication. Instead, it's an invitation to realize that at its best the main component of communication is an ever-changing mutuality of commitment—an interdependence which bolsters the effectiveness and the satisfactions for participants. It is because interpersonal communication is so connected to relationships rather than to individuals that it is so beautiful, mysterious, frustrating, confusing, exciting, wondrous, ambiguous, and human.

Learning, Caring, and Other Educational Matters

Though it seems clear to me that effective interpersonal communication and effective education should depend upon the same set of concepts, you and I have consistently structured communicative insights out of campus and classroom relationships. We are lured by the efficiency of impersonality, objectivity, "knowledge," and "respect" for role differences. Learning, teachers and students implicitly tell each other, primarily results from the interaction of teaching and studying—but surely you can see what is left out of that formula. You are. Your uniquenesses, your emotions, your motivations, your personness. Learning can't be *that;* we can't let it be.

Lasting learning isn't something you receive in schools. You develop it in response to your perception of your environment just as communication patterns are developed. Lasting learning isn't just intellectualized and filed away for future reference. It is lived, with all the implications summoned up by that word. When you really learn something, it is integrated into your personal style rather than layered on, paper thin, ready to be torn, yellowed, stripped off, or covered over by time or later layers.

I'm seeing that the best way for anyone to talk about learning is to talk about his or her own learning. So, what I'd like to stress in recalling my own experience with learning to learn is the essential congruence of learning and communication as concepts. They are the same process, despite the absurdist educational structures which deny such a fundamental truth. "All too often we are giving our young people cut flowers when we should be teaching them to grow their own plants."[8]

I've made five observations recently about my own learning, in schools and out. I am not ready to claim they're universal, profound, or even terribly original. But they *are* mine. Since I can accept that

---

[8] John W. Gardner, *Self-Renewal: The Individual and the Innovative Society* (N. Y.: Harper Colophon Books, 1965), p. 21.

education as communication

"learning" may be different for you, I invite you into my meanings and hope you'll contribute yours in response.

Observation 1

What I've really learned has inevitably changed me and is continually changed by me

That which hasn't changed me much may be a recognized fact, stored, subject to recall, perhaps retrieved; but to apply the term "learning" to my memorization of the date Eli Whitney invented the cotton gin (he did, didn't he?) seems like gross distortion. If I haven't decided something is important enough to alter my image of the world significantly, I haven't learned it even if I remember it. Volume after volume of technical literature in education has been written comparing conceptual approaches to learning theory, but to me the truest learning is simply the art of discovering and being open to new meanings. To do this, I have been over the past three or four years increasingly willing to risk my images of the world in a creative act of journeying. I've been rewarded for my own efforts *by* my own efforts. And I've changed in ways which fold back on themselves and will redirect the course of my future learning.

Psychologist George A. Kelley is somewhat more general in his approach, but consistent, I think, with my observation: ". . . learning is not a special class of psychological processes; it is synonymous with any and all psychological processes. It is not something that happens to a person on occasion; it is what makes him a person in the first place."[9] It is, in short, communicative. Students are persons if they truly learn. They learn if they are truly persons.

Observation 2

My best learning has both "act" and "attitude" facets

If the change in me has been a growth change (and I'm convinced it has) then the change in my behavior as a result of it will be apparent to others. I'll be trying out new behavior in new circumstances—the "act" dimension of learning. But this new behavior will likely be ineffective unless I add an "attitude" dimension consistent with my action. For example, self-disclosure is a valued concept for me; I try to stress it in my interpersonal communication classes and elsewhere, and am becoming increasingly open to others as a result of implementing it. But I some-times hear myself self-disclosing in a conversation partly in order to

---

[9] George A. Kelley, *A Theory of Personality: The Psychology of Personal Constructs* (N.Y.: W. W. Norton, 1955), p. 75.

students as real people

"open up" the other person. My disclosure becomes in a sense a tool for a personal end, a manipulation. I have set up a situation in which the "act" of self-disclosure is accomplished without the slightest deference to the trusting and acceptant attitude which must accompany growthful disclosure. Similarly, I can identify the conscious actions I need to undertake in order to learn something I suspect will change me beneficially (psychomotor skills, acquisition of new knowledge, etc.) but unless I simultaneously develop facilitating attitudes and appreciations, the skills and knowledge will hardly benefit me. The two dimensions complement each other and, taken together, provide impetus for the individual searching for personal growth.

Observation 3
My best learning has been built, not received

Our language serves to deceive here. Throughout my life I've said "I'm in school to get an education." When I didn't understand something well enough, I said "I don't get it." Teachers asked me, "Is it getting through to you?" Peers wondered, "Did you get anything out of that class?" I knew that model children at home were "seen, not heard." Political speeches and academic lectures were later "delivered" to me. I "got" an education, I figured, like I "got" a Christmas present, or "got" a summer cold—passively.

Gradually I learned (!) that no one else was capable of giving me *my* education or *my* learning. It had to fit me and they simply didn't know me well enough. They could help, they could direct, they could intimidate or cajole or encourage, but they couldn't give it to me because it would then be phony. Listening to and parroting back Professor X's interminable biology lectures didn't give me my education; it gave me X's education warmed over. Some might be satisfied with that brand of less-than-real learning. I was then. I'm not now.

But I can't create my learning alone. Ultimately, learning is a "we-process" like communication; it is participative. Through you I see me, and through my interaction with friends I have glimpsed a potential me which I have partially learned to encourage. The two-wayness I'm referring to here—so clearly and directly a part of communication—takes varied forms. It might be no more complex than a willingness to ask questions from the back of the lecture hall, or to participate fully with peers to learn without course-related coercion. Personal growth requires dialogue and multilogue. My effective learning has come when I can sense my connections with others and act on them, when I look to the relationships for clues rather than looking singly to who *he* is, who *she* is, or even who *I* am.

education as communication

Observation 4
I have often learned significant things as a result of crises, confusions, and irritations

A crisis unresolved demands learning, as does a promise unfulfilled, a potential unsatisfied, anger unexpressed. Choosing how to express the anger, satisfy the potential, fulfill the promise, and resolve the crisis sets the stage for my learning, but only if I'm clear on how it's me who does the choosing. I have consistently been "off balance" and frustrated when I have learned. Not long ago, I promised a student I'd bring one of my poems for her to read. I forgot, then forgot again. She reminded me and I even forgot again. I was embarrassed and angry at myself since it could have looked like I was playing at being coy and modest. I finally learned something about myself by observing myself in a frustrating situation: I seem to be very protective of my writing and fear negative reactions (perhaps especially from students and females!). But at the same time I crave acceptance, which got me into the situation in the first place. Chances are the situation will recur, and maybe—maybe—I will learn to risk myself more.

Observation 5
My learning often occurs as a result of letting things happen rather than trying to make them happen

A class a couple of years ago got off to what I thought was a very slow start. I didn't look forward to going and neither did the students. But they still came; attendance was surprisingly good. I gradually, grudgingly, took more and more responsibility for class directions, supplying more and more structure and increasingly focusing my worries on what I was going to say in class. I began to resent what I perceived as the class daring me to be entertaining, expecting me to be a performer. I didn't appreciate that and finally confided my resentment to the class. In the discussion which unfolded, I learned something about myself from some people's perception that I'd introduced the class as a brand of manipulation—that the group *would* be informal, that we *would* be close, that we *would* be open with each other, that we *would* become a community. Although I had meant my opening remarks to the class to be predictive, using past experience as a guide, I seemed to be guilty of trying to make things happen in education rather than discovering them in process. Often the goals a teacher wants most in a class will be subverted if he or she consciously tries to structure them into a plan. This particular group reacted as most would to what they saw as a threatening

students as real people

dare; they withdrew. Interpersonal participation picked up only after we mutually realized that neither my dare ("you will be open and close") nor theirs ("you will perform for us so we can remain uncommitted") was satisfying.

M.C. Richards tells quite a story about the same idea:

As I grow quiet, the clay centers. For example, I used to grieve because I could not make reliably a close-fitting lid for a canister, a teapot, a casserole. Sometimes the lid fitted, sometimes it didn't. But I wanted it to fit. And I was full of aggravation. Then a GI friend of mine who was stationed in Korea sent me an ancient Korean pot, about a thousand years old. I loved it at once, and then he wrote that he thought I might like it because it looked like something I might have made. Its lid didn't fit at all! Yet it was a museum piece, so to speak. Why, I mused, do I require of myself what I do not require of this pot? Its lid does not fit, but it inspires my spirit when I look at it and handle it. So I stopped worrying. Now I have very little trouble making lids that fit.[10]

I am reminded of all the times students work so hard to learn material for an upcoming exam. If it's important enough to your grade point average, scholarship, or admission to law school, you will stay up night after night with coffee and pills and notebooks with blurring words and incomprehensible doodles, recalling lectures that never interested you and reviewing a text you never really wanted to read in the first place.

Not all learning is easy—don't get me wrong. It often demands intensive and basically unpleasant study. But the notebook words won't unblur until you supply a reason to yourself why the material applies to you and you can appreciate and care for your relationship to it. Then you won't need to try so hard. Then you have been freed and you're more likely to allow learning to take hold. The lids, as M.C. Richards would remind us, will start fitting better.

Learning in Schools

Overall, my conclusion is that learning most often occurs as a result of a nurturing or facilitating *environment,* but rarely occurs as a result of a teaching (or learning) *strategy.* Strategies are defense-producing and distance-producing phenomena because they won't let you be "in charge," following your own interests at your own pace.

Learning might profitably be thought of as unrestrained caring— caring for oneself, for the other, for the subject matter. You might

---

[10] M. C. Richards, *Centering: In Pottery, Poetry, and the Person* (Middletown, Connecticut: Wesleyan University Press, 1962), pp. 22-23.

education as communication

sometime analyze your learning environment according to the extended treatment of caring in Milton Mayeroff's little book *On Caring*.[11] He dissects the concept so well, so completely, and so gently in under a hundred pages that you might find yourself nodding in silent affirmation and underlining almost every page as I did. Caring to Mayeroff is basically a communication relationship, as is the educative process to me.

Alternative Models of Educational Responsibility:
A Summary

The idea that education should be observed with the same criteria as interpersonal communication—that education really is communication and vice-versa—will be reflected in the schools if we are to become all we can be. But on most college campuses I've observed, a different philosophy prevails.

Students are sometimes considered by themselves and others as products of the system, as though college is a factory in which they are assembled for later worthwhile use in "the real world." Different departments in the factory, of course, do different things to you, to give you "marketability." The nagging drawback to this view is, of course, that you are dependent upon the skill of others in putting you together and you know too much about quality control in the modern factory to feel much at ease. Regarding education as something done to you is not only a cop-out on your own responsibilities to recognize the control you can exercise over your life, but destroys the interpersonal dialogue necessary for effective learning.

As an alternative, education is sometimes considered a place where you purchase a product which you can then use to your own advantage. I call this the "K-Mart model of education," because it requires so little involvement and so much plasticity. But you're not a "consumer" of education; that view cops out by transferring responsibility, too. It's too easy to take a defective toaster back ("It's K-Mart's fault").

Actually, if we insist on economic analogies or models of education, I'd suggest an innovation that has popped up here and there across the country for fixing your car. Education from the student perspective could be analagous to driving your car into a fix-it-yourself garage where you pay to have access to the proper tools, materials, environment, and probably advice from a qualified mechanic on duty. But your car is fixed by you. And once you decide that education is more like this garage, you have begun to accept responsibility. You *care* about your car because you care about your safety and pride and those who ride with you. What is

---

[11] Milton Mayeroff, *On Caring* (N.Y.: Harper & Row, 1971).

students as real people

the motivation to cheat, to cut corners? ("I'll cheat and not replace as much brake fluid this time." Who is cheated?)

Economic or mechanical analogies, though, are misleading if they dehumanize. The human interaction factor is the critical part of education, so it might be possible to justify a "lover model of education." Sounds better already, doesn't it? The other models, the "factory model," and the "K-Mart model," especially, imply education is something either built into you or supplied to you. These are one-way approaches, anticommunicative and dominated by the thinking of monologue. But education is not *reception*, it's *conception*. Just as lovers conceive something new and unique out of the interaction of that which exists now, students and faculty can conceive ideas to maximize human potential if they care to. The caring must be mutual and the meaning of the caring shared.

4.

listening
as
other-affirmation

Four questions seem to be asked consistently in higher education, nonverbally if not verbally. More often than not, the inquiries are barely beneath the surface, waiting to emerge if an audience seems receptive. But only in rare and unguarded moments does a student or a teacher become a real and affirming audience for another person at school, perhaps because he or she suspects the answers to the four questions will be negative.

Higher education—if it is really "higher"—should provide "yes" responses to these questions: Do you notice me? Will you try to understand me? Can you see why I'm important? Will you help me realize my potential? I've written in another chapter that communication involves two general facets, giving opportunities and taking others into account. Positive answers to the first two questions give people the impression they're being given an adequate opportunity for communication, while positive answers to the last two will convince individuals they're being taken into account.

Some things can stand repetition. *The most lasting message of all education should be a clear "yes" to the questions, whether they're overtly stated or merely implied.* A student once remarked to me that college was a jail into which he had forced himself. Our observation as we talked about it more: just as inmates don't especially care who serves time alongside them, many students tend not to pay any attention to each other, aside from small friendship cliques. And just as jailers don't especially care who is behind their bars, many faculty and administrators tend not to take into account the uniqueness and worth of students. For my friend and so many others, the questions weren't answered, nor were they acknowledged as questions worth asking in the rhetoric of the campus. Ignorance of the questions is a powerful, and frustrating, answer to the questions.

41

students as real people

We desperately need ways to affirm others in education. We desperately need ways to convince ourselves that what we're doing is important, and that we're doing it with important people who *can help* and *need help* at the same time. I believe it's possible for you to find such ways, so in the next two chapters I'll ask you to be sensitive to topics you probably have already considered in communication, but be sensitive to them in slightly different ways. I'm anxious for listening to be considered important not just for instrumental or self-serving purposes, but for other-affirming purposes as well. And I'm anxious in the following chapter to explain why honest messages in interpersonal communication can reflect and stimulate the best in people and not, as many think, degenerate into put-down sessions or depressing termination of relationships.

A Personal Note

I'm sometimes tempted to describe one of my days by saying "I didn't get anything done; too busy listening to students." There have been a lot of those days. Every time I sat down to read class papers or schedule the next Academic Standards Committee meeting or write a placement service recommendation or revise my syllabus for next quarter, a voice would say, "Have you got a minute?" Thank God there are a lot of minutes, even when they become hours.

I consistently resist the temptation toward cynicism because I'm aware that my criteria often get fouled up and I lose sight of what I am and what I am for. Talking and listening with students is what I should "get done," what I'm about as a teacher. Saying "yes" to being a listener is more pressing than what seems a compulsive desire of teachers—professing the world out of its problems.

Part of my problem might be that I enjoy listening so much that I distrust its usefulness as a way of spending time. My culture has taught me two things in this regard. What I do for mere enjoyment probably wastes time, while what I force or "discipline" myself to do will probably be more valuable in the long run. The latter choice is supposedly more likely to produce tangibles, and is clearly more in line with work ethic thinking. Enjoying listening to students is an immediately suspect activity with which to fill my day, both internally and (I imagine) to my neighbors who punch out after eight to ten hours at the steel mill.

But the process of listening is finally attracting some long overdue academic and popular attention, attention which can lead to no other result than a more complete conception of humane communication. That's important, for listening is the subprocess which most directly affects the quality of oral communication situations; that is, it determines whether the meaning generated in one person by a message is more or

listening as other-affirmation

less congruent with the meaning intended by the other's utterance of the message. Has the meaning been shared? Indications are intertwined, but the answer may lie in how well the participants have listened much more than in how well they have spoken. The complexity of listening has led researchers very naturally to specify the effectiveness of differing styles of listening and correlate it to a series of personality and situational variables. Though I am not averse to that approach, I don't intend to pursue it here. Rather, I'd like this chapter to point to what I perceive as a neglected direction in our thinking on listening which, if explored, could lead to the further humanization of our lives. I'll attempt to indicate that direction after a brief examination of what may be identified as the main current emphases in discussing the concept.

Functions of Listening Behavior

Students of human speech for centuries concentrated on the word-as-spoken, on how to make it more beautifully expressed, more pleasant, more pragmatic, more conducive to the attainment of power, more in congruence with "reality." The impetus to studying communication was the desire to adopt an effective personal style of expression. Though listening was always an implied necessity, we waited until the 1940s, according to one analyst, for scholars to begin to consider the receptive aspects of communication through serious speculation and research.[1] But the narrowly pragmatic rationale for studying communication did us a disservice when it was transferred to the newfound interest in listening processes, since it forced us to focus on those behaviors which help the person become a better listener enroute to successful (that is "acquisitive") living. Such a rationale locked us into a view of listening behavior which seemed to permit only three major functions of listening.

Information Reception

This, of course, is the model of education with which we often constrain ourselves. The successful students are the "good listeners," the ones who have learned that the retention of lecture material is highly rewarding. Similarly, the anecdotal accounts of listening improvement in business and industry gave rise to and are consistent with the efficiency claims of, for instance, the audio tape Xerox listening program. Personal reward follows the accurate reception and recall of verbal message content. It's a truism and I don't intend to argue with it, though I doubt its value warrants all the attention it's received.

---

[1] Carl Weaver, *Human Listening: Processes and Behavior* (Indianapolis: Bobbs-Merrill, 1972), p. 23.

students as real people

Empathy

Here, too, is an admirable function, one which has been unjustifiably slighted when compared with the preceding function.[2] Its importance resides in the very definition of communication as a sharing of meanings. Empathy is the means by which a listener establishes a direct if inferred emotional contact with another in relationship—commonly described as a "feeling with" rather than a "feeling for" the other. In empathy, I attempt to take the perspective of the other person, recognizing his or her distinctiveness and allowing for it in my responses. We need as much research as we can get into the mysteries of empathic thought and action, and again, my purpose is hardly to discourage such interest. Listening to establish empathy is crucial.

Critical and Discriminative Capacities

The effective listener is able to discriminate truth from falsehood, sincerity from deceit, the real from the sham. He or she can analyze, divide an issue into constituent parts, and criticize from a rational base the applicability of social messages. Larry Barker's recent *Listening Behavior* devotes an entire chapter to "Listening to Biased Communication," and it's a good one.[3]

Each of these functions and its attendant behaviors has generated impressive bodies of research and equally impressive lists of advice and skills designed for individual improvement. All are pretty much dependent upon what the listener *does* after he or she chooses to listen, and all relate essentially to effects in the listener. Depending, of course, upon your value system, they probably will make you a better listener. But given this preponderance of attention devoted to the mechanical skills of listening, I've grown more interested in the question of whether you *choose to become a listener,* and the effects of that choice on an interpersonal relationship.

I claim that the choice-to-listen is an important communicative unit of analysis. As an interpersonal decision, it may be the most important in the relationship because it has as its most obvious effect the affirmation of the other's existence and worth. I feel a need to expand from an emphasis upon what listening does for the respondant to what *being listened to* does for the initiator and the relationship.

---

[2] Charles M. Kelley, "Empathic Listening," in *Small Group Communication: A Reader,* Robert Cathcart and Larry Samovar, eds. (Dubuque, Iowa: William C. Brown, 1970), pp. 251-259.

[3] Larry Barker, *Listening Behavior* (Englewood Cliffs, N.J.: Prentice-Hall, 1971).

listening as other-affirmation

Affirming

One of the major purposes of human communication is simply more communication. Each message so intricately and necessarily sets the stage for those which follow that this function is obviously more important than the short term effects and reactions stimulated by an individual utterance. Life is drama, all right, but at any given moment, the "lines" could be said to be more a part of an "overture" or "prologue" than the play itself. This precedent quality and function provide evidence for what I see as an important insight about communication; that it is a fundamentally pleasurable activity. We communicate to obtain facts, we communicate to understand, we communicate to attain power, we communicate to relate; all these are certainly true and undiminished by my claims. But mainly, we continue to communicate because it is fun to do so.

Communication is so pleasurable because through it we are noticed, we are taken into account, we are bolstered in our belief or hope that we as individuals are important.

I realize I'm worth something when I have something important to say. And I realize I have something important to say primarily when others are willing to listen. Recognizing my own worth is not an internal process; social interaction provides me with this information and it's my reaction to it that convinces me that I'm a person. In effect, I'm *affirmed* by the choice of others to notice me and react to me. I make a social difference, therefore I am.

Similarly, I can choose to facilitate the same recognitions in others, and the process of listening is my vehicle. In this reaching out, I'm operating not from a strategy, but rather from an urge; effective communication is pleasurable to me. The other-affirming listener validates the value of the individual person (the other *and* self) and the value of the social relationship.

Three elements seem most valuable in understanding listening as other-affirmation—availability, choice-to-listen, and confirmation.

Availability

Being available[4] for the initiation of interaction is an often neglected social message on an overt level, but seldom unnoticed. It's a psychological readiness with physical manifestations you and I have learned to observe. I walk into a colleague's office and can tell (or think I can) from his behavior-in-situation whether he is available; whether

---

[4] See John Keltner, *Interpersonal Speech-Communication: Elements and Structures* (Belmont, California: Wadsworth, 1970).

45

students as real people

there will be a forum for my wants or needs. The unavailable teacher is perhaps a memorable example for most of us. Several of mine structured their duties so as to arrive late and leave immediately following classes, scheduled late afternoon office hours, made continual reference to overriding personal commitments and business, or in myriad other ways made clear to me that their problems didn't relate to my problems and my needs didn't relate to their needs. By being unavailable, they disaffirmed the importance of students before any opportunity to prove otherwise through personal contact. The system of expectations was closed.

Too often we speak of "openness" as only an *outgoing* activity or frame of mind. We sometimes act in this culture as though the only open person is the one who freely and honestly expresses whatever is being felt as it's being felt. This person makes open or lets out what is in. But just as an open door lets things out *and* lets them in, the concept of openness in communication must refer equally to those who freely and honestly are ready to be accessible to and accept the disclosures of others.

Being available is an invitation, and the basis of the invitation is this message: "I won't make decisions for you; you're capable of deciding when you need to initiate an interaction. But when you decide to initiate, I'll try to be here for you." This availability cannot of course be a guarantee any more than an open invitation to visit my house is a guarantee that guests will be embraced enthusiastically whenever they drop in and whatever their actions. Rather, the invitation indicates to the others that they are recognized and valued, that they make a difference, and that barring unusual circumstances, I welcome their presence. A climate of availability is an important first step to significant interpersonal affirmation, and provides context for specific further actions which signal choice-to-listen.

The Choice-To-Listen, Freely Expressed

I'd like us to become accustomed to considering the act of listening as a message itself with profoundly humanistic value. We often don't.

Sam Keen has stressed in two recent books that each person has a story to tell.[5] Primitive man caught glimpses of his place in the continuity of existence and culture by participating in shared myths, legends, and stories. A sense of history was maintained by the same process through which individuals were integrated into their culture. Persons developed

---

[5] Sam Keen, *To A Dancing God* (N. Y.: Harper and Row, 1970); Sam Keen and Anne V. Fox, *Telling Your Story: A Guide to Who You Are and Who You Can Be* (Garden City, N. Y.: Doubleday, 1973).

listening as other-affirmation

a sense of identity and in-placeness by being able to tell a personal story reflective of a collective story, and by being exposed to the stories of others. But modern culture's technological preoccupation invalidates personal storytelling as an important activity. History is "transmitted" and personal identity supposedly found through other means. The oral storytelling tradition has been lost, Keen believes, but a reclamation of it would serve humanity well in getting us back into touch with ourselves.

The most important step a person can take in this regard is "granting permission," an act analogous to what I term the choice-to-listen. Keen writes:

> Each of us has a story, but few have had audiences before whom it was appropriate to share intimate and meaningful history. Some, whether from wisdom or illness, have gone to professional listeners, such as therapists and clergymen, and have received permission to tell who they were and who they hope to become. However, our culture does not ordinarily provide a forum where the stories of individuals are shared.[6]

All of us continually come into contact with others who have stories to tell, and our choice is whether we will become an audience, thereby helping the other to explore with mutual benefit what may be ambiguous territory, or whether we will remain in a private and therefore futile groping for our own amorphous stories.

Many, of course, make the choice-to-listen, but not freely. Situational requirements often seem to mandate a pose of listening, a mask worn without commitment. What they have actually made is a choice-to-hear (if that). "Hearing" describes the ear's reception of stimuli; "listening" the internal commitment to make sense of them, to try to build out of them a sense of meaning shared with the other. Listening is the active translation of another's overt speech into the silent speech appropriate to inner existence.[7] It is possible to adopt the physical trappings associated with being attentive—the inclined head, the inquiring expression, the occasional nod—as a stop-gap measure to give the appearance of listening. Some of my attempts at such fraud have been discovered on the spot; the unmasking of others has been longer in catching up to me. But catch up they have, and the sadness of it all arises from the mutual embarrassment of my being caught and the other being insulted. I had ignored someone under the guise of immersing myself in them, and that

---

[6] Ibid., p. 72
[7] Charles Brown and Paul Keller, *Monologue to Dialogue* (Englewood Cliffs, N. J.: Prentice-Hall, 1973).

47

students as real people

kind of insult is hard to take. It would have been more helpful for me to have admitted my preoccupation with other matters, admitting why I could not at the time fully commit myself to a choice-to-listen. To have done otherwise was a severe disaffirmation of the other.

Confirmation

In this chapter, I've meant to use "affirmation" with a basically value-laden connotation. I am affirmed by you if you make public a positive assessment of (though not necessarily an "agreement with") my personness, if you somehow recognize and accept my potential as a person. But Joseph Luft reminds me of a similar and perhaps less value-associated term:

> ... the act of interpersonal confirmation is of special importance. To confirm one another is to authenticate as valid how we perceive each other. It means to give some degree of certainty to that previously regarded as doubtful. It is one of the most important ways of alleviating anxiety. Interpersonal confirmation means concurring on interpersonal perception. There is the relief that comes with corroboration of what one is, what one thinks, and what one feels. One is even strengthened to the point where one need pay less attention to what one is and release energy toward what one can become. In short, to confirm another person is to enhance his prospects of growing in line with his potential.[8]

Confirmation, then, is not saying "that's good" or "that's right," but saying "that *is*." As such, it is a necessary element in the process of affirmation, exhibited in the tendency of the listener not just to receive but to respond, to clarify, to inquire if necessary. I listen not just with my ears but also with my questions and my feelings. The confirmation says in essence, "you have been heard; here is how I understand your statement." Rogerian response styles and popular approaches in parent-child communication proposed by Ginott and Gordon are basically confirmative.[9]

As Luft implies, each confirmative act frees the other to "go on from there," to realize that the relationship is an environment open to change and the trying out of new behaviors. Confirmation helps both participants stretch, even if they don't want to stretch in the same direction.

---

[8] Joseph Luft, *Of Human Interaction* (Palo Alto, California: National Press Books, 1969), p. 136.

[9] For examples: Carl Rogers, *On Becoming A Person* (Boston: Houghton Mifflin, 1961); Haim Ginott, *Between Parent and Child* (N. Y.: Avon Books, 1965); Thomas Gordon, *Parent Effectiveness Training* (N. Y.: Peter H. Wyden, 1970).

listening as other-affirmation

Listening and Student Culture

When I was an undergraduate, I usually assumed I was a good listener. Going to lectures was, while not fun, at least easy for me. The jottings and doodles in my faded and dog-eared spiral notebook usually sufficiently indicated future test questions. My ears were alert for academic clues telegraphing what might later be an exam. Correct more often than not, I noticed myself becoming an academic commodity among my peers, sought more for advice on what to study than why it needs to be studied or (God forbid!) what I thought personally about what we were studying.

Though listening for information is important, I obviously no longer believe it is the most important type of listening in which students can engage. From the student's point of view, I now see three reasons why listening to affirm is more helpful.

First, educational systems are escaping from the philosophy that the best education is totally objective, that human emotion contaminates one's rational development. Education is becoming increasingly interactional and value-centered, emotionally as well as cognitively satisfying. People who feel unimportant, though, are not effective value-clarifiers for themselves or others. And people who are not affirmed by the educational environment will almost invariably notice nothing valuable for them to clarify while they are in school.[10]

Second, students are often asked to present oral reports in class in both individual and group situations. But I've noticed an occasional problem in maintaining a receptive audience. During one term, attendance, participation, and interest levels aeemed high during the part of the quarter in which I was primarily responsible for suggesting activities and topics, but dropped noticeably when *student* groups were scheduled for presentations. People seemed to work well with their own groups, but were surprised when they came to class on their big day to confront a significantly smaller and more apathetic audience than expected. The problem, as I now say to classes when I get irritated enough, is that students are not in the habit of respecting themselves as teachers with something to say and as learners with needs they—as students—can fulfill. Please don't try to cut my pay because of this, but I can't help but believe that most of the significant things you learn in college should be learned by interaction with other students rather than through the teacher-pupil pipeline. "The fact is," writes Harold Taylor, former president of Sarah Lawrence College, "That the latent power of teaching—

---

[10] You might be interested in looking through Sidney B. Simon, Leland W. Howe, and Howard Kirschenbaum's *Values Clarification* (N. Y.: Hart, 1972). It is representative of a whole range of relatively new materials which assume students bring their whole persons to school.

49

students as real people

teaching considered as the influence of one person on another—lies in the student body and not exclusively or necessarily in the teacher. At the present time, that latent power is untapped."[11] Educator Arthur W. Chickering is even more to the point: "A student's most important teacher is another student. Friends and reference groups filter and modulate the messages from the larger student culture. They amplify or attenuate the force of curriculum, faculty, parietal rules, institutional regulations. They can trump the best teacher's ace and stalemate the most thoughtful or agile dean."[12] The unwillingness of students to recognize this, and the unwillingness of faculty and administration to encourage it, sometimes leads to an additional reason to improve listening on campus—simple loneliness.

An example of this third reason, the potential disconnectedness of campus life, occurred not long ago at the beginning of a quarter. An ex-cheerleader from a large local high school remarked that before finding herself in an interpersonal communication class, she was ready to quit school. Having been on campus for over a quarter, she was amazed at how disconnected she felt, at her difficulty in starting relationships and in maintaining the friendships begun in high school. People seemed to change in college to her, becoming less interested in each other while emphasizing wholly private goals. They seemed, she said, to take isolation as the normal state of affairs on campus. Her attempts at conversations were so consistently rebuffed that it became clear that her choice was either to conform to the norm of loneliness or leave, renouncing the values society ascribes to a degree and renouncing personal ambition as well. She is staying, at least for a while, and beginning to make contact. But too many people don't come into contact with others who have made the choice-to-listen. Too many aren't affirmed by being noticed as unique and valuable individuals. The Committee on the Student in Higher Education found that often ". . . self-doubt, self-rejection, self-hatred, and self-punishment become almost endemic to the collegiate culture. Feelings of rejection and worthlessness, although they may be obscured by a veneer of poise and sophistication, occasionally incapacitate the student and frequently impair his real abilities."[13]

The person who feels there is no real listening audience for his or her important messages is faced with two choices—either an elaborate rationalization for the empty silence of life ("I function best as a loner") or the attempt to gain the attention of others through unconventional means.

---

[11] Harold Taylor, *Students Without Teachers: The Crisis in the University* (N. Y.: McGraw-Hill, 1969), p. 225.

[12] Arthur W. Chickering, *Education and Identity* (San Francisco: Jossey-Bass, 1971), p. 253.

[13] The Committee on the Student in Higher Education, *The Student in Higher Education* (New Haven, Connecticut: The Committee on the Student in Higher Education, 1968), p. 24.

listening as other-affirmation

I am both amazed and afraid when I listen to Harry Chapin's song "Sniper," because it takes me on a journey into the head of a twenty-five-year-old man who made the second choice.[14] Based loosely on the 1966 Charles Whitman incident in which people were shot at random from a tower on the campus of the University of Texas at Austin, the song weaves together a communicational analysis of why we need to be listened to and what can happen if we aren't. Murmuring background voices at the beginning of "Sniper" are requesting "talk about me, talk about me, talk about me. . . .," but the answer is "not now, not now, not now. . . ." The sniper decides that if others ignore him so easily, he must say or do something which cannot be ignored. So Chapin builds an elaborate communication metaphor, by taking his rifles and ammunition up the tower, Whitman is preparing for his "conversation." As he starts firing, the song describes the shots as words, questions, messages. When someone is "questioned," or has "gotten his message," they have been shot. An "answering call" describes the return fire toward his position. The sadness of the song for me lies in the inevitability of the event; Whitman, who had never been satisfied before that he was being heard, had to convince himself that he *could* be heard by a tragically extreme message. But only the scale needs to be changed to bring Whitman's feelings into my own life.

When I'm ignored by a close friend, I usually find a way to get him or her to notice me, and the way I find doesn't always help the relationship. When the parents of a fifteen-year-old boy don't listen to him as though he has worthwhile things to say, the teenager will make the parents hear *something*. The overt message may be stolen cars, drugs, "undesirable" friends, constant lateness getting home, or a variety of other statements, but the underlying message is often the same—"I'm not being listened to, but you'll *have* to listen to this. . . ." Whole nations, of course, act this way, and it satisfactorily accounts for the identity-seeking activities of many social groups in the past fifteen years or so. How could students be much different?

The answer, not a complete one, but pretty satisfying nevertheless, is for us to recognize each other's humanity by giving the most important and affirming compliment it is in our power to give: the message that the other is valuable enough to listen to.

Loneliness can be countered if people are willing to try to improve their communication. All three of my reasons for urging more listening in colleges are summarized in this experience of a professor:

One day when I said "What's on your mind?" the class fell into an extra long silence, as if caught by surprise. Miss Edick, who had frequently launched the class into a good discussion, started to speak, looked sad and confused, and then said in low voice, "I don't

---

[14] In the Elektra album "Sniper and Other Love Songs," EKS75042.

students as real people

know—this may sound awfully strange. Maybe I shouldn't ask, but I've had to think about death lately, and I just wonder what you think of it."

She looked around the room as if expecting instant wisdom and I thought, "My God, this will be a terrible session. What does she expect us to do with that question on the spur of the moment?"

There was another long pause. Miss Edick started to mumble apologies again. No one laughed at her. Then one student said she supposed we didn't worry as much about the fact of death for ourselves as what we should do when others lost someone close to them. Several agreed. I brought up the notion I had read recently in Walt Whitman, that before birth we are unconscious and not in pain at not being alive, but are part of a universe preparing for us. He was hinting, I said, at what someone else had told me recently that if we do not suffer before birth, we probably will not after death; and therefore the state of nothingness that is death is not to be feared.

Some students agreed. One said he felt unworried because he believed in an afterlife. He spoke without belligerence, and another student said calmly he did not believe in an afterlife and therefore did not worry about death.

At this point I was sure the class would choose up sides and the religious war would rage. But no. The students continued to put before each other their notions about death, and Miss Edick listened. Finally, she said "Thank you," and the discussion was over. From the first, the others had sensed her mood, serious and sad, and respected it. A week later she told me her father had been informed he had cancer and only three months to live.[15]

Though I see no point in convincing myself to affirm all your actions (I'm too opinionated for that), I can't avoid seeking ways to affirm the essential humanness in you, the potential for what we can become if I am simply aware of three elements of listening as other-affirmation. I need to be available to you, ready to encounter you and your issues should you decide to initiate. I need to make a choice-to-listen after you initiate which is sincere and facilitative in the telling of your personal story. Finally, I must be willing to confirm "your you"—when I learn it—by sharing and comparing "my you." This, too, is a facet of listening, though few consider it so. I see in Dominick Barbara's statement a capsulization of the perspective toward which I'm striving:

---

[15] Ken Macrorie, *Uptaught* (N. J.: Hayden Book Co., 1970), pp. 177-178.

listening as other-affirmation

Communication becomes more effective as we see and listen to others as they appear realistically. It is essential that we see others as unique personalities, with beliefs, thoughts, and wishes of their own, whose capacities for thinking and experiencing are constantly changing, growing, developing into something new and stimulating. Genuine understanding is dependent, above all else, on this *eagerness to affirm the integrity of others.*[16]

---

[16] Robert Oliver and Dominick Barbara, *The Healthy Mind in Communion and Communication* (Springfield, Illinois: Charles C. Thomas, 1962), p. 93.

5

honest messages
as
other-affirmation

(R)Evolution

Something is happening, and I'm trying to let myself understand what it might mean. It's not just something happening to me, not just a personal change, although it's created many of those and will continue to do so. The "it" I'm referring to is ambiguous enough for me to be uncomfortable in attempting description, but real enough and important enough for me to make the effort. It's flowing around me while I'm looking for a label to attach, a handle to grip, a structure in which to fit myself. But the labels seem imprecise, handles nonexistent, structures so diverse and shifting that a single perspective provides no justice.

I frankly don't know if I'm referring to a genuine social revolution. This word "revolution" has been so oversaid and undermeant recently that, like the listeners of the little boy who cried "wolf!" too often, we may be justifiably suspicious of each new fervent prediction of social revolutions or "new eras." But the wolf *does* come to call sometimes, and what are we to tell ourselves?

Indications are gathering that, revolution or evolution, wolf-like or lamb-like, the future of our culture will be fundamentally different than even our immediate past. It will perhaps become more *our* culture than before, more the result of positive identifications of persons who transact with and help to transform the culture than members who feel trapped by it. Culture is us, together in here; not somewhere out there.

Some of these indications of change appear obvious from my perspective as an educator. Around me I see an increased interest in humanistic enterprises of all sorts. Encounter and sensitivity approaches appear to have achieved a solid and respectable maturity as a more balanced, realistic assessment of their potential has replaced both unrestrained ecstasy and unreasoned attack. Social criticism and the behavioral sciences seem to be emphasizing increasingly a new sense of individual human *choice*. The future in education and elsewhere is

54

honest messages

increasingly seen as open possibility rather than stifling inevitability. Technology, the ogre of futuristics a few short years ago, is more and more understood as a freeing agent which will allow us the social space and energy to exercise meaningful choice. Concern for integrity and openness in public life seems to be on the upswing, as are methods of participative and supportive management in industry.

In tandem with such changes, I'm noticing an encouraging reception on personal and institutional levels to what I term "acceptance education." Acceptance education is dialogue-based and dedicated to welcoming cultural diversity while seeking through mutuality the connections necessary to take advantage of it. Mutual senses of cooperation imply acceptance-of-self, and here too I'm encouraged, as I hope you'll see in this chapter.

Generally, it is the concept of *the person* around which clusters future possibilities for our culture. We are constructing an informed vision of what persons are for and how they can better create interdependence with other persons. *The person in relationship* is where social action begins and where its consequences are felt. And *person* in today's culture is less an isolated biological entity than a social, communicational, in-motion, self-constructed and self-realized bag of potential.

This realization feels good. It means that you and I exist at a time in which our efforts can help expand the outline of humanness. We do it by affirming each other, by calling attention to that which is good, unique, satisfying, and helpful, in each other and in ourselves. But we need to recognize we also affirm personness by a constructive acknowledging of that which frustrates, saddens, angers, and perhaps darkens.

I've written this chapter from a vantage of optimism that our future is a place where honesty in human relations will not simply persist, but will thrive as a social criterion in a way never before anticipated. It will thrive not because it's always pleasant, but because the risk of its unpleasantness is our only avenue to knowing and surviving.

This new culture of honesty must thrive. I cannot be affirmed by your deception, and you cannot be affirmed by mine. And we want very much to be affirmed.

This does not, and cannot, mean that affirmation always means agreement.[1]

---

[1] Several books have been especially important in influencing my understanding of the future of our culture. They include George B. Leonard, *The Transformation: A Guide to the Inevitable Changes in Humankind* (N. Y.: Dell, 1972); Thomas Hanna, *Bodies in Revolt: A Primer in Somatic Thinking* (N. Y.: Dell, 1970); Fred Richards and Anne Cohen Richards, *Homonovus: The New Man* (Boulder: Shields, 1973); Charles A. Reich, *The Greening of America* (N. Y.: Bantam, 1971); Phillip Slater, *The Pursuit of Loneliness: American Culture at the Breaking Point* (Boston: Beacon Press, 1970); James H. Craig and Marge Craig, *Synergic Power: Beyond Domination and Permissiveness* (Berkeley: Proactive Press, 1974); Erich Fromm, *The Revolution of Hope: Toward a Humanized Technology* (N. Y.: Bantam, 1968).

students as real people

Affirming by Trust

Trust as Prerequisite

Perhaps the most important result of those relationships in my life which are particularly close and effective is an increased level of genuine trust. Strangely, the same factor, trust, was in many ways a prerequisite for the formation of those relationships. There exists a tragi-comic cycle of human behavior in which you and I don't communicate well because I don't trust you enough to be myself around you. I don't trust you because I don't know enough about you. I don't know enough about you because you haven't been yourself around me. You haven't been yourself around me because you don't know enough about me. When you don't know enough about me, you don't trust me. Because you don't trust me, you and I don't communicate well.

Poor communication feeds distrust, and the cycle accelerates toward superficiality and/or despair. Worse, the cycle is inevitable if we accept its underlying assumption that a person must be feared until he or she proves otherwise. Indeed, this seems to me to be the basic assumption of technological culture and the basic contributor to the alienation we often feel. But a radically different model of humankind is not only possible but available, gathering momentum. Its impact, as I suggested earlier, is already being felt.

This model affirms our basic desire to offer trust from the beginning in a relationship, thus breaking into the cycle, opening the way for an authentic level of communication attainable not just by accident or crisis but by "normal" social patterns.

My reaction to such an idea some years ago would have been something like: "That looks okay on paper, I guess. But it's really stupid, because real life just doesn't work that way." I thought that especially in education, real trust was pie-in-the-sky idealism. There's a game to be played: not a fun game, but a necessary and inevitable one. On with the game. I don't accept that anymore.

The TORI Approach

I recently participated in two community-building workshops convened by psychologist Jack Gibb. Each was based on what he and his wife Lorraine have termed "TORI theory,"[2] and each opened for me a fresh

---

[2] Clear introductions to TORI, an acronym constructed by stressing *trust/openness/realization/interdependence*, are found in Jack R. Gibb, "TORI Theory and Practice," *The 1972 Annual Handbook for Group Facilitators*, ed. J. William Pfeiffer and John E. Jones (La Jolla, California: University Associates, 1972), pp. 157-162; Jack R. Gibb and Lorraine M. Gibb, "Role Freedom in a TORI Group," *Encounter*, ed. Arthur Burton (S. F.: Jossey-Bass, 1970), pp. 42-57.

honest messages

sense of the possible in human relationships. To Jack and the other members in these essentially leaderless groups, I feel tremendous gratitude. Each provided for me a unique growing opportunity and in each I found myself responding in fresh and loving and satisfying ways. I responded in freeing ways, I might add, which surprised me and divulged "new" facets of me which always must have been here. I'm now beginning to see the implications of TORI as a life style, not because of an artificial "high'" injected over a weekend and dissipated when I emerged into the stark reality of the "real world," but because of the persistence of a series of simple realizations about my life.

I don't need to control others to be happy. I don't need to "win" arguments, either, or mistrust, be independent (or dependent), seek to change others, "play my cards close to the vest," or invent needless rules to substitute for meaningful communication with you. I can, if I'm willing to let go of some of my fear, allow myself to (1) trust others, (2) open myself to their messages while giving them access to my feelings as they're occurring, (3) realize my personally formulated goals of growth by being free to experiment with new behaviors, and (4) be interdependent with—fully "with"—others by permitting and validating our mutual freedom. Thus the acronym: *T*rust, *O*penness, *R*ealization, *I*nterdependence.

This idea is not important to me because of some attainable communication skills unique to TORI theory. It's important to me because of the opposite—my increasing suspicion of techniques and systems of communication improvement skills you can buy on the open marketplace from the Answer Merchants. TORI doesn't seem to be a technique for better living, but rather a description of the essence of fully human and fully liberated living. Being in the world in a way entirely consistent with our nature and needs as humans, but in a way we've had to persuade ourselves was impossible because of competitiveness, divisiveness, rules, roles, and social systems. It's not impossible, the Gibbs seem to suggest from over twenty years of research into the behavior of healthy human groups, because TORI is synonymous with essential life processes and all we have to do is get out of their way (remove undue reliance upon roles and rules, etc.). To the extent you and I are role-free we can communicate as persons, honestly and affirmingly. Role-bound, we cardboardize ourselves, letting the role or the underlying rule talk in lieu of the sensitized inner self.

Think about the roles out of which you operate and confront the world. A role might be considered to consist of those actions you've programmed and performed again and again in a relationship because of your expectations and/or the expectations of others. How many of your female friends only know you in your role as the cool, imperturba-

students as real people

ble, detached, strong, worldly provider? How do they get access to the little-boy part of you that skips merrily through the rain and wants to cry in the sad movies? Are you genuinely you around your mother, or do you adopt the role of loving daughter (or rebellious daughter, or. . .)? Would your mother profit from seeing the whole range of your personality expressed occasionally, instead of just that part she expects to see, or that you feel safe in showing? Do your teachers have access to *you*, or just a sterile representation of the don't-step-on-any-toes mask you assume (maybe you have a "surly student," a "sweet young thing," or an "egghead" mask instead)? When you talk with me out of class, is it still your role talking with my role? If so, is it any wonder we both leave with that unmistakably empty feeling that discourages further interaction?

A student told in class recently of her belief as a young child that teachers lived in their school desks. That got a big laugh and seems delightfully ludicrous, so I recall my experience while in junior high school of seeing my biology teacher (soon to become principal) buying *liquor* in a drug store. I couldn't see the person for the role; couldn't accept that he had a life independent of my shallow contact with him. (Where did I think he lived?) If he *drank*, did he *get drunk?* And if he *got drunk*, did that mean he had *feelings*, too? Very disorienting. I could never dismiss him again as easily as I'd come to dismiss other teachers. There was a depth to my experience of him from then on, a silly and distorted depth, but depth nevertheless. Occcasionally, I've invited smaller classes to meet in our home, and, while I may be imagining it, they also seem to display some of this disorientation in a kind of dismay that our tub has a ring in it, that last night's dishes are sitting unwashed and starting to stink a bit, that some underwear got left on the hall chair. We sometimes sweep away role residue very reluctantly. At least I can prove I don't live in my desk.

Many of you will choose careers of teaching at some level and will be forced to discover how to respond to this role-reliance and nondisclosure in education so as to retain your sanity. Good luck. Teaching is certainly a role, and students certainly often respond first to the role and second (if then) to the person in the role. This hurts sometimes, but maybe not as much as realizing that we teachers have encouraged the perception in the first place.

Though some roles are probably inevitable, your choice is whether you can reduce reliance upon them. So much of that reliance is based on fear, the antiagent of trust and the barrier to my being interpersonally what I am personally. Yes, I risk a lot by renouncing the safety of my roles around you. I have no guarantee you won't make fun of me, hurting me, or find a way to take advantage of the nakedness of my end of our communication. A favorite book of many of my students is John

honest messages

Powell's *Why Am I Afraid to Tell You Who I Am?* In it Powell reports this actual conversation:

> *Author:* "I am writing a booklet, to be called *Why Am I Afraid to Tell You Who I Am?*"
>
> *Other:* "Do you want an answer to your question?"
>
> *Author:* "That is the purpose of the booklet, to answer the question."
>
> *Other:* "But do you want *my* answer?"
>
> *Author:* "Yes, of course I do."
>
> *Other:* "I am afraid to tell you who I am, because if I tell you who I am, you may not like who I am, and it's all that I have."[3]

I have nowhere to retreat if my risk is unrewarded by your understanding.

But you can know that; that's open information in our relationship if I choose not to rely on a masking role or a power role. I've exhibited a choice/risk which opens our relationship, breaks into the cycle of distrust, and clears the way for a wider variety of honest messages. But the central message of this sort of choice/risk is an affirmation of the value and the trustworthiness of the other person. "If I love someone," says psychologist Sidney Jourard, "not only do I strive to know him; I *also display my love by letting him know me.*"[4]

Openness: Both Ways

Receptivity and Acceptance

I'd like to return to a topic of Chapter 4 and treat it in a somewhat different manner. It's important because of how often "openness" is discussed only in terms of how verbal a person is, how glib, how easily he or she can divulge their history or feelings. The open person is sometimes assumed to be one who indiscriminately tells and tells and tells regardless of the needs of the listener.

But openness has another dimension to balance this more obvious outgoing aspect. Openness exists also in my orientation to and expectations about the outside world. If I desire, I can structure my expectations so as to make much of the environment conform to me. If I expect you to be hostile, my defenses are aroused, my guard is up, you notice that, interpret me (accurately) as already hostile toward you, and thus tend

---

[3] John Powell, *Why Am I Afraid to Tell You Who I Am?* (Chicago: Argus Communications, 1969), p. 12.

[4] Sidney M. Jourard, *The Transparent Self* (rev. ed.; N. Y.: D. Van Nostrand, 1971), p. 5.

students as real people

toward expressing hostility at this "unfair" behavior of mine. My expectations were closed, and our two person system became closed to the potential we both could have recognized.

I have a wide variety of behaviors I can choose in my relationships, but most of them fall into one of two categories; I can be in those relationships either *inviter* or *challenger*. Only through invitation do I gain access to the unfolding you which can help me grow. And true invitation accepts the world and the other as it/he/she is—I am receptively "open" without stipulations or qualifications. I invite you to my house, I don't dictate what you will wear; I invite you to a class, I don't tell you when you can or cannot talk; I invite you into dialogue, I don't tell you what is permissible to say. To behave otherwise would be challenge disguised as invitation, closedness masquerading as openness. True invitation implies acceptance which grants and respects freedom, especially the freedom to decline the invitation.

Verbal and nonverbal contributions to interpersonal invitation cannot just be classed as "incoming" openness. Invitations have message value—*affirmative* message value—even when they remain unaccepted. Accepting people as they are without any attempt to change them to fit my expectations affirms them and connects them with me—not because of anything as shallow as agreement, but acceptance responds eloquently to the more important need of people to make a difference in their world, to be understood.

Carl Rogers has written perceptively of this relationship between understanding and acceptance:

> *I have found it of enormous value when I can permit myself to understand another person.* The way in which I have worded this statement may seem strange to you. Is it necessary to *permit* oneself to understand another? I think that it is. Our first reaction to most of the statements which we hear from other people is an immediate evaluation, or judgment, rather than an understanding of it. When someone expresses some feeling or attitude or belief, our tendency is, almost immediately, to feel "That's right"; or "That's stupid"; "That's abnormal"; "That's unreasonable"; "That's incorrect"; "That's not nice." Very rarely do we permit ourselves to *understand* precisely what the meaning of the statement is to him.[5]

I have found that truly to accept another person and his feelings is by no means an easy thing, any more than is understanding. Can I really permit another person to feel hostile toward me? Can I accept his anger as a real and legitimate part of himself? Can I accept him when he views life and its problems in a way quite

---

[5] Carl R. Rogers, *On Becoming a Person* (Boston: Houghton Mifflin Sentry Edition, 1961), p. 18.

60

honest messages

different from mine? Can I accept him when he feels very positively toward me, admiring me and wanting to model himself after me? All this is involved in acceptance, and it does not come easy.[6]

Teachers need to learn not to respond to students with closed expectations but with an opening receptivity to their needs. Too often, we've responded only to our needs in deciding to change students into what we think they need to become. Especially in classes stressing communication, this cannot be the ethic. We've judged and evaluated consistently in lieu of attempting to accept and understand where students really were, and their definitions of where they needed to go. My classes, for instance, have often been (consciously) challenges, acting at least implicitly as dares to students that "you probably won't be able to grasp what I want you to know, but you'll be a lot better off if you could. I'll sit in judgment and tell you when you've arrived or how far you have to go." There is no meaningful invitation there, no affirmation. There is a snubbing of you and a paranoid and dishonest elevation of me. I believe you are justified in feeling angry with teachers who do this, including me, as you recognize the times in this book when I've been unable to shake the biases of my role.

Of course, your friends also may be justified in feeling anger when some of the same biases show up in your behavior through judgmental reactions to them. If even positive judgments elicit defensiveness in relationships,[7] you might consider yourself as a source of unnecessary judgments as when have you responded evaluatively when you might have accepted? (With teachers? Other students? With me, here?) When have you tried to change another person to satisfy your needs, or worse, merely your wants or preferences?

Rogers and others suggest a method of checking your openness to experience which has enormous potential. It involves the commitment to try to see the world as the other person sees it, and is implemented by nothing more complex than our assumption that we are different people and that our differences have to be noted and accepted before we can begin to build any meaningful relationship. "Active listening"[8] is at work when I preface my response to a significant message from another by making sure I understand it as nearly as possible *the way it was meant to be*

---

[6] Ibid., pp. 20-21.

[7] Jack R. Gibb, "Defensive Communication," *The Journal of Communication,* 11 (September, 1961), 141-148.

[8] Carl R. Rogers and Richard E. Farson, *Active Listening* (Chicago: University of Chicago Industrial Relations Center, 1957); Thomas Gordon, *Parent Effectiveness Training* (N. Y.: Peter H. Wyden, 1970).

students as real people

understood. I can do this by focusing first not on my own feelings, which is irresistibly tempting at times, but on the message itself:

> "I think you're saying that the test was much too tough for a General Studies course."

> "You feel disappointed because your comment in class was apparently ignored."

Listening actively can also take the form of checking back on the other's meaning by responding to observed behavioral components of a message:

> "I've noticed you seem to be comfortable in a class which has almost no formal structure."

> "I'm hearing a lot of rational arguments, but mainly I'm seeing the tension in your face as you talk about this grade. I'm interpreting that as anger."

Clearly, listening in this way involves more effort (and tentativeness) in a relationship; I am responding not just to *content,* but often to the *feelings* which accompany and perhaps motivate the choice of a particular set of words. I must respond, in fact, not just to words, but to the myriad nonverbal indicators which embellish your messages. It all becomes worth it when I noticed that my checking back helps you to become more expressive and open with me. I have not cut you off with my immediate judgment; I have expressed my willingness to explore your world of meaning. If my inferences are incorrect, I have extended to you the opportunity to correct me, and I expect to be corrected.

Active listening is preliminary to empathic, compassionate understanding—the only genuine way we connect with each other in the world. "All knowledge of another person is real knowledge," says Erich Fromm, "only if it is based on my experiencing in myself that which he experiences. If this is not the case and the person remains an object, I may know a lot *about* him but I do not *know him.*"[9] When Fromm claims that "every person carries within himself all of humanity,"[10] he indicates to me that we have the resources truly to understand each other, but they are often like our natural resources, either unnoticed or squandered.

---

[9] Fromm, p. 82.
[10] Ibid, p. 83.

honest messages

Listening by checking out the other's meanings might get to be tiresome if you're trying to do it after every comment you hear. My experience has been that it's especially valuable when used judiciously, as to develop a "license to disagree" with another. A speech teacher once told me I had to develop a "license to speak" in public: before I presumed to take up the time, energy, and attention of an audience, I had to be sure of what I was saying and sure I was prepared to say it. My license was my preparation. Surely he won't mind if I borrow his idea to suggest to you that if I disagree with you *without inspecting your meanings from your perspective,* out loud, in both content and feeling dimensions, then I'm disagreeing without a license and probably wasting our time. My license is my sincere effort at empathy. Only when I understand your versions of honesty can I be effective with mine.

Disclosure and the Emotional You

Most serious students, as students, seem to deny they have feelings at all. This isn't surprising, given the educational system which goes out of its way to establish a vicious message, here interpreted by a student:

They keep telling us in high school, a freshman is a quarter of a person, a sophomore is a half a person, and by the time you graduate you're four quarters of a person at last. *Then* you can have some respect. But we still have our *opinions,* and no one's opinion is wrong, because it's their own personal opinion.[11]

Paradoxically, after you've endured this "completing-yourself" process and wish to go on to college, you're starting from scratch again. Perhaps in college you'll confront an even stronger attitude that you're not a whole person with opinions and feelings to be heard and respected. I've noticed that in most college contexts, authority group expectations (trustees, administrators, teachers) tend to be accepted passively by nonauthority groups (students and staff). Students are so often forbidden to respond even on the relatively uninvolving "head" level at which education is usually pitched that it should not be surprising to find that your feelings *about* what you're doing are even more taboo. To "them" *and to you.*

So you guard your feelings with care, though some part of you knows that you and others at college—whatever the role—would like to be comfortable with open feelings, and, more crucial, would like to be able to say so when uncomfortable.

So rarely does a genuine feeling surface in class that it probably signals an *event* in your school life. The other day, I showed a videotape

---

[11] Gerald Weinstein and Mario D. Fantini (eds.) *Toward Humanistic Education: A Curriculum of Affect* (N. Y.: Praeger, 1970), p. 201.

students as real people

in class of a well-known educator discussing aspects of love in interpersonal relationships. Afterward the discussion focused on how "effective" it was, how "true," how "applicable." How safe we were, how unemotional and analytical in response to a presentation which warned us about overanalyzing and not trusting our emotions!

I was surprised during our discussion to hear from a student who had only rarely addressed the whole group during the previous class meetings. He, too, made a positive comment, safely and ambiguously worded, but made it with such intensity that something told me there was more there. So I asked, "John, how are you feeling right now?" Total silence, from John and the entire group. Several times during the next twenty or thirty seconds, John appeared ready to begin a response, but each time thought better of it and retreated. No one interrupted. I believe we all sensed the depth of his struggle. Finally, tentatively and softly, he said, "I'm wishing I had someone to care for."

No one commented for another thirty seconds or so. I believe we were all connected by the impact and simplicity of his feeling—by the impossibility of an elaboration or analysis of it.

I'll remember John for a long time for his gift to us which took so much strength, a gift saying "I feel safe enough with you to risk sharing a real and wrenching feeling."

I believe that for that moment he realized that genuine disclosure means choosing to *be* on the outside what is *felt* on the inside. Not for selfish or cathartic reasons but for relational ones. So that one may be understood as fully as possible. So that, as Camus puts it when referring to disclosure to those we love, we don't have to be ". . .revealing ourselves in order to seem but in order to give."[12]

I'm concerned that my disclosure to you will be judicious and relevant, since only then will it operate as a gift. I am not interested in telling you everything I feel all the time. That would tire me out, if not endanger me or bore you in other ways. I value my privacy and value my choice to disclose or not disclose, to pick my places and times. I realize, however, that my rights to this sort of choice have to be balanced against your rights in our relationship, and in seeking this balance, I'm sometimes led to disclose when it's painful to both of us but healthy for the bond we build together.

Choosing to Disclose

If you choose to be more of a discloser in educational or other personal contexts, I predict you'll notice four exciting things happening to your relationships. First, you'll notice yourself becoming more re-

---

[12] Albert Camus, quoted in Joseph Luft, *Of Human Interaction* (Palo Alto, California: National Press Books, 1969), p. 58.

honest messages

sponsive to the rights and needs of others around you. Genuineness in disclosure always demands an assessment of the potential effects of the disclosure. I've noticed that many if not most of the emotions I've hidden from my students are matters they have a right to know, given the ways we've defined the relationship. It's mistaken for me to believe "my" emotions affect only me; if they get in the way of me understanding you, then you're affected profoundly, and, more important, our relationship is affected.

One example comes to mind immediately, and it happens to be something which is a bit painful to me. I have never required attendance in my classes, a fact which has been noticed and appreciated on a variety of levels. I've never considered it particularly as a problem, but certain people have liberally advantaged themselves of a policy (I had congratulated myself) which treated students as what they are—responsible adults, with choices of their own. In response to people cutting class, I've usually maintained my cool and accepting image: "It's your choice; makes no difference to me. . . ." Several times, when such students came to me later in the term with special problems and mentioned the fact that they'd not been in class much, I'd haul out that liberal, accepting mask and put it on, pretending that it really made no difference to me as long as it was a personal choice. To those of you who may be reading this as former students of mine: if you're out there, and remember, I want you to know it made a difference to me. My feelings were often hurt when you missed a lot. I often felt slighted, belittled, frustrated, and, I have to face it, angry. I realize this isn't terribly consistent with my philosophy of teaching, but it's there. I need to apologize to you because when you came to me with your special needs, I was hearing you through a veil of my own hurt feelings which I denied even to myself. But in a sense you may have had a right to know about them because you were affected. Although I have a choice not to reveal them (which I exercise often), and though I take full responsibility for them, I cannot assume that I'm the only one affected by "my" feelings. In a relationship, my feelings are our feelings, and if possible you should have access to them too. Since I've begun to consider disclosure in this way, I've become more aware of what the interpersonal rights of others might be, and how they interconnect with my rights.

The second change in your relationships might be that, as a discloser, both you and the other will increase your resources for discovering identity. Disclosure is the process of providing both the other and yourself with the raw "data" of the relationship. It is not just a giving with no return, since the giving in disclosure is the return, for by talking, you learn about yourself, your interests, and your capacities. Lyndon Johnson as Vice President is reputed to have displayed a sign in his office

students as real people

announcing, "You Ain't Learning Nothin' When You're Talkin'!" Although my understanding of Johnson in retrospect throws some doubt on whether the sign was a general pronouncement or a specific warning to visitors, it suggests at face value a relatively misleading view of communication. More realistic would be Wendell Johnson's approach, in which "your most enchanted listener" is always *you:*

> If we would understand a man by his words it is best that we listen to what he says when he is either in trouble or in love. For if we do, and if we are quiet and attentive, we will notice that no matter how fully he may be taken over by the illusion that it is to us he speaks, he talks at such times most surely to himself.
>
> Pondering this, we come in time to realize that every speaker is his own most captive listener.[13]

It is you, listening to you, as you interact with me, that develops in you a notion of who you are. And, of course, it is you, listening to me, as you interact with me, that helps to develop in me a notion of who I am. Indeed, William Heard Kilpatrick long ago observed that "consciousness of self and consciousness of others emerge simultaneously to the individual, each growing and contributing during the rest of life mutually to round out and implement the other."[14]

Conditions of disclosure also aid the exploration of attitudes toward others, a critical dimension of self. Daryl Bem's approach to self-perception suggests that it's not just our attitudes which influence our behavior; our actions toward others—as we perceive them—will exert a powerful influence on the attitudes we hold concerning the others.[15] The implications for trusting and honesty in relationships are obvious. As I notice myself behaving in trusting ways toward you, I begin to infer that I like you more. As I notice myself shrinking from you, avoiding you, I infer that I fear you. Disclosure brings such issues into the open, creating new channels for us to discover our respective identities.

Third, you may find that being more overtly honest with your emotions will free you to exercise more control over those emotions. Not long ago, I asked students to respond to this question: "What is the relationship between expressing emotions and controlling emotions?" Almost every answer identified these as opposite ideas; controlling emotions meant keeping them hidden inside, while expression was often

---

[13] Wendell Johnson, *Verbal Man: The Enchantment of Words* (N. Y.: Collier Books, 1965), p. 22. This book was first published in 1956 with the title *Your Most Enchanted Listener.*

[14] William Heard Kilpatrick, *Selfhood and Civilization: A Study of the Self-Other Process* (N. Y.: Macmillan, 1941), p. 2.

[15] Daryl J. Bem, "An Experimental Analysis of Self-Persuasion," *Journal of Experimental Psychology,* 1 (1965), 199-218.

66

honest messages

equated with a recklessness regretted later. I shouldn't have been surprised. No doubt many have had such negative experiences with emotional openness, and no doubt the educational environment facilitated the brand of response I received, in that closedness in schools tends to be safe and openness can be dangerous. I say I shouldn't have been surprised, but to be truthful, I was. To me, talking about my feelings increases my chances of remaining in control of them. Brown and Keller present impressive evidence that the habit of verbalizing emotions "builds into ourselves our own mirror" or emotional response possibilities which can later be used to reflect back and sort out our understandings in new experiences.[16] Having "control" is largely a matter of exercising *choice* over how, when, and to whom they'll be expressed. The person who maintains total emotional secrecy has denied choice and thus is just as much out of control emotionally as the person who flies into inappropriate tantrums. I may be in control of my car when it is in my garage, but I am also in control of it when I am displaying it to others, or when I use it to help a friend move across town. The basis of control is choice, and the habitually closed person has relinquished an important avenue to increased self-understanding. I know a woman who bought such a nice car that she was afraid to take it out of the garage. There it sat, as she, in a very real sense, had denied herself control over it and allowed it control over her.

Finally, your emotional openness will tend to validate and encourage openness in others. I mentioned earlier the cycle of mistrust where inadequate knowledge of the other serves to prohibit the risks you'd like to be able to take in relationships, but fear too much. But we are all fearful; we are all looking for connections; we are all grateful for understanding and the sincere attempt to understand us. I used to tell myself that I could be the kind of me I wanted only if I could be sure others would accept that openly. I now realize that they weren't any more free than I was to respond openly, unless I help by giving them an indicator of safety. This indicator paradoxically almost has to be "the kind of me I want." And it has to be a real sharing of self. Since I've discovered as a teacher that I can be more human in the classroom, relying less and less on role, students seem much more human and individualized to me. They teach me more about communication because they respond as humans, not roles. Sure, closedness seems to be a cycle, a reciprocating activity. But just as surely, openness is also a cyclic, reciprocating, self-reinforcing process.

Reciprocation is facilitated when I combine in my behavior both the desire to let part of me "out" and the desire to be as openly receptive

---

[16] Charles T. Brown and Paul W. Keller, *Monologue to Dialogue: An Exploration of Interpersonal Communication* (Englewood Cliffs, N. J.: Prentice-Hall, 1973), p. 87.

students as real people

with you as possible—when I reflect both outgoing and incoming aspects of openness. My outgoing honesty has to be *provisional* and *personalized* because I'm aware I often am not as in touch with myself as I'd like; my self-understanding is literally a process, always changing and developing into something different. My incoming receptive openness, if it's honest, has to be *provisional* and *personalized* also; I'm aware I see the world through my own set of filters and distortions.

Therefore, I can't speak for the world or for you. I can only speak for me. Most of my statements about our relationship demand an "I-orientation." I find this hard, though, since I've been taught so long that one doesn't use "I" too much for fear of being thought self-centered. But in terms of communication theory, I am literally self-centered, and cannot be anything else. But I do have the choice not to be self-centered in an absolutist and impersonal sense. I don't want to be tempted constantly to shift the weight of responsibility for me onto you. "'I-messages" encourage honesty; "you-messages" encourage cop-outism.[17] You haven't caused what's in me. I cause it, by creating inner interpretations of *your* actions perhaps, but the source is ultimately *me*. The sooner I learn to reflect this insight fully in my outgoing openness, the better our communication is likely to become. I am in the process of regaining my "I," which was partially robbed from me by my formal education. Good luck with yours.

Regaining the "I" in interpersonal talk is a major factor in developing an openness style which is supportive. There are others, all interconnected. As I implied earlier, I am consistently most comfortable around those whose response styles are basically nonjudgmental. They have not imposed their standards on me. They encourage me to form my own reasons. They allow me to be, while alert to the natural differences they see in me simply because I'm a process, becoming. They are not afraid to tell me those differences as they notice them, not to satisfy their needs, but to let me have as much data as I deserve to make my decisions, to meet my needs. They let me feel I am not in competition with others for their favor. They let me feel at ease even when making mistakes. Their presence makes embarrassment bearable. *Noticing*, not *judging*, is their model of feedback, and I love them for it. But others, the judgers, see the world in a different, rank-ordered way. Their feedback (I don't particularly like this word) is really *fed* back to achieve personal goals and to use me as object. Their responses do not support me or our relationship. I once wrote a whimsical poem about this kind of attitude, so prevalent in schools. Sorry for the indelicate allusion, but it wrote itself before I could stop it:

---

[17] See Chapter 2 for an elaboration of this concept.

honest messages

As feedback
Gets fed back
I get fed up

Hunger should be preceding
Feeding

I'm full

Feel free
To be
But remember to see
In me
The need
For food for thought
But no need
For your spoonfeeding

I never digested a thought
I didn't pass somehow
That didn't fertilize something
(Aren't all ideas basically shitty?)

But what are we doing
Feeding each other, anyway?
Even though the menu
Is inevitably potluck
I'll choose, thank you
I'll use me
While you
Choose and
Use you

We each have a spoon
Let's partake together
Share together
Cook for each other
Spoon as lovers

But
As feedback
Gets fed back
I get fed up

students as real people

Closely allied to a nonjudgmental style of being open to others is an unconditional attitude. A group of students and I recently agreed upon the amazing impact of the word "no" in both family and school life. The word has been used so much it loses some of its contextual significance and takes on a kind of symbolic connotation around which clusters widely varied impressions. "If" is the same sort of animal. You are "accepted *if*" your ideas are submitted in the proper form, observing bureaucratic protocol. In much the same way, my words in the classroom seem somtimes to be accepted *if* they constitute testable material, glossed over or ignored if they do not. But please, notice that occasionally teachers speak seriously from the heart, in class, without planning a trap for you.

Unconditional acceptance applies to people, of course; not to ideas or behaviors of people. I don't suggest that you be an undiscerning or uncritical listener to messages. I'm only reporting that I've felt better since I stopped constructing conditions which the other person must meet in order to retain that precious and golden commodity, my friendship. If you have to take a test each time you consider whether our friendship continues, then the strain we both will feel will probably diminish us. I have friends with whom I disagree strongly and accept lovingly. I find ways (I hope) to express my differences without implying that they need to change to retain my friendship.

I am interested in learning. But a most effective way to keep me from learning is for you to maintain lofty standards of "tact." Much of what goes under the label "tact" in our culture necessitates shielding me from your feelings about me while you're experiencing them. Because you're frightened, you decide for me that "Rob can't take it; it'd be too much for him." How can you decide that for me? I can agree that timing in disclosure is important, but the next time you're tempted to be tactful, stop and consider: whom are you protecting the most—me, or yourself? Disclosure of strong feelings as they are experienced and where they are experienced (a "here-and-now orientation") is with relatively few exceptions the approach which leads to better understanding. Sam Keen in *To a Dancing God* calls to mind the connections among three words, all spelled the same.[18] The "present" is *now.* If I'm "present," I'm *here.* If I'm fully open at present in the present, then I have given you a *gift* of incalculable value—a "present."

Education seems to run on questions as an engine runs on gasoline. Questions everywhere—true-false, multiple choice, course evaluations, discussion-starters, inquiries about the margins for the term paper, "when are your office hours, again?," "don't you think that test was

---

[18] Sam Keen, *To a Dancing God* (N. Y.: Harper and Row, 1970), p. 27.

70

honest messages

unfair?" Overall, I'm a big fan of questions. But I'm aware of how often they are used as statement-camouflage.

The person who has found a facilitative style of openness weighs each question he or she is tempted to ask to check whether there isn't a statement about feelings which would be more helpful to all parties in the relationship. Sometimes my questions merely mask confusion, and perhaps that shows through clearly enough. Other times, they insidiously mask stronger and more subversive feelings like anger or frustration, and it is then when my responsibility should take over for my fear. Once, when students were particularly silent while we (I) "discussed" a topic which I had perceived as interesting to the class earlier in the quarter, I heard myself inquire, "You said you wanted to get into this— do you really?" I can't begin to express on paper my tone of voice; it rang even in my ears as a challenge from superior to inferiors, calculated, I guess, to stimulate guilt, but probably not producing anything except defensiveness. I'm not sure, but I think I followed this up with a barrage of other questions ostensibly designed to get us "back on the track." What happened, of course, was that I was angry that I'd spent so much time preparing materials to follow up on what the students had identified as an interest, and kind of hurt that they hadn't had the courtesy or courage to tell me previously that I'd misread their level of commitment. I didn't have the courage to disclose this, though, so I fell back on the tried and true educational tactic of hiding behind questions. It's so hard to say "I'm hurt," and so easy to say "Don't you think that. . . .?" I'm learning.

(R)Evolution and Change

I have just scrapped the fairly complex organization I had planned for this concluding statement. That's hard for me to do, for this chapter is to me one of the more important things I've written lately. But I don't think you'd have as much interest in that other conclusion as the way I'm about to summarize.

All I'm saying here is that you have choice; that your life is your life; that in schools your communication can either be real or sham; that educational sham manifests in roles much more than in malicious deceit; that emotional openness in both directions repays itself and validates its own risks; that your style of openness affects your perceived openness; that honest messages do affirm others, and yourself; that vulnerability is not only possible, it is strength.

Finally, a few words about the (r)evolution of which I spoke at the beginning of the chapter. A student friend recently expressed some despair at what she saw as the increasing apathy among current students

students as real people

when compared to the vital activism of the 1960s. I too, see a diminishing of participation in large social movements, and to some extent, less identification with "causes." I cannot interpret this as apathy, though. Not when I talk constantly with students who are strongly committed to exploring their personal resources of identity, love, and giving. I am encouraged and enlightened by an increasing personalism or, perhaps more appropriately, interpersonalism, which motivates students to a newfound sense of growth and responsibility. They understand that it is in the informal communication relationships of our lives where we can effect the most social change by giving ourselves as real listeners and real people. I immerse myself in the evidence daily in personal journals, conferences, even term papers and exams.

I was a college student from 1963 to 1971, observing and sometimes participating in my small way in that era's style of activism. I'm a latecomer to the (r)evolution of interpersonal dialogue.

Again, though, I'm learning.

6

the ecology of academic audiences

Our Audienceness

I believe that sincere people are often so busy trying to understand each other as speakers that we lose sight of the fact that we need to understand each other as audiences, too. I need to listen to your speaking, but you need to speak to my listening, as well. The effort of speaking to the other's listening, that is, considering the other as a fully functioning audience with unique listening characteristics, which must be taken into account, is one of the most difficult and crucial tasks in interpersonal communication.

College and university life provides both formal and informal interaction with groups of differing communication values and assumptions. These values and assumptions become so easily solidified into expectations of repeated behavior—roles—that we'd better start making allowances for each other's audienceness *out of role*. Mark Gauss, a student writing in my introductory course in interpersonal communication, saw this clearly and, in the process, saw a person where before he had only seen a role:

From the first day of class in my U.S. Constitution course, the instructor came in, stood at the lectern, and read his notes. I did not care too much about what he said (and most people cared even less), especially his opinions, because I had no empathy with him (it wasn't because he was boring). How can you have a feeling for, or care about a lecture robot? No one can be empathetic with a machine. But one day he came, and went to the lectern like usual. But instead of lecturing like always, he said, "I am really tired," and walked to a chair in the back of the room and sat down. He told us about a dream he had the night before. He had dreamed he was

73

students as real people

giving a lecture in class, but there were only two students present. As he went to leave, he found that his shoes were nailed to the floor. He talked about his past (he had taught at a prison, and was scared of his students, at first). He also gave us his feelings about the area. It was great. Now the classes are better, even though he still lectures, because it's more personal. I can have empathy with a person who I know has funny dreams, gets scared, and tired.

Believe me, it's difficult for a teacher to make this commitment to speak as a person to the listening of other persons. It's much easier (I've been here, too) to speak as a role/robot to the automatic responses of other role/robots. But a strange phenomenon often occurs with the commitment. As we disclose our differences to each other, our striking similarities become clearer, too. And empathy, the ability to take the other's perspective on the world, makes interaction more fulfilling and meaningful.

Of course each of us is a speaker in our communication environment. But I've noticed that the quality of relationships is perhaps more profoundly influenced by our mutual "audienceness," our mutual granting of permission for the other to speak. Stated simply, our characteristics as audiences *for* each other in higher education become at least as important as the content of what we have to say *to* each other. The latter, if anything, depends on the former.

The Importance of Understanding Audience

A time-honored way of examining public communication has been to assume that the rhetoric of individuals can influence large audiences to change behavior. Thus, research came to be focused upon the techniques employed by these individuals—their specific effectiveness, general power, ethics, persuasive strategies, and so on. The not-too-hidden assumption of this approach is that audiences are created and swayed by individual leaders, and that audiences are important primarily as indicators of the power of those leaders.

In schools, I've assumed until relatively recently that the leaders and shapers had to be the teachers, the audience (shaped) had to be the students. Only becoming a teacher showed me the extent to which teachers must become an audience to the leadership of students.

I've also wondered if I could revise my outlook concerning the importance of audiences. Perhaps, taking a revised perspective, it's the audiences in our social systems which tend to influence most directly the nature of rhetorical effect. The shifting flow of an audience coalescing into a recognizable unit is the chief rhetorical event of our time, and it often seems to happen without the conscious guidance of individual

ecology of academic audiences

leaders. Indeed, communication analysts may have been looking 180 degrees in the opposite direction all these years. Instead of individual communicators shaping and changing audiences, a more suitable model might be to think of the presence of audiences as suggesting shapes and changes in the individual rhetoric of public communicators. More likely both are true—the effects are interactive—but there's little doubt in my mind that communicators need to look much more to the *effects of* identifiable audiences rather than for *effects in* those audiences.

I'm presuming here that you're committed in some degree to becoming a better whatever-you-are, or a better whatever-you-are-becoming. If I'm wrong, and you've read this far, there's probably not much point in continuing to read. You'll not be an effective audience for me, and I don't have the opportunity here to be a direct audience for you. If you and I are committed to learning in higher education and not just to biding time, we need to consider closely the styles of academic audiences and their effects on student, faculty, and administrative speech.

Campus Relationships:
I Am a System, You Are a System, We Are a System

I've let too much of my thinking be rigidly shaped in terms of partness rather than wholeness. This extends to treating people as if they were separate, walking, talking brains. People are not just brains with bodies and emotions possessed and attached, though; we are, to borrow a word popularized by William Schutz, "bodyminds"[1] unified into our existence by all our personal resources. And just as clearly to me now (why did it take so long for me to realize this?) people are not essentially cut off from each other; we are together unified into our existence by a common realization that understanding is an interpersonal resource.

It might help us to notice that each of us is a *system* composed of a variety of components, each of which has functions. The alteration of any of the functions or any of the components cannot help but affect the entire system. The system is whole when components and functions interact harmoniously preparing the system to (1) interact with other systems, and (2) become effectively functioning components of larger systems. So, each of us is simultaneously system and subsystem, whole unto ourselves and sustaining component of something larger. A problem in part of me affects *me*; a problem in me affects *us*; a problem in us affects *all of us*. "No man is an island" thinking is appropriate here, but is not very prevalent on college campuses.

---

[1] William C. Schutz, *Here Comes Everybody: Bodymind and Encounter Culture* (N. Y.: Harper and Row Harrow Books, 1972), pp. 1-13.

75

students as real people

Elements of a system are interdependent. They can never change independently without effects being perceived throughout the system. Human changes similarly cannot be merely dependent, or one-way. Persons in relationship exist by transactions, or mutual definitions of each other. Who I am with you interdepends with who you are with me. Each of us selects our messages in response to the audiences we perceive, and former professors Don Robertson and Marion Steele say:

> Sometimes you just have to laugh and sometimes it hurts too much to laugh. For when you look around and all the time you see education that prevents learning, and campuses that prevent community, and students who don't care if they learn anything, and trustees who want learning to be orderly, and administrators who want education to be neat and computerized, and teachers who keep students from learning the things that are important to them (and pretend to do it for the students' own good), and classrooms designed for maximum control and discomfort—when you keep getting blasted in the face by contradictions as glaring as these, you just have to laugh, or wince or scream as loud as you can.[2]

I'm not sure about you, but my feelings are not as bitter as those behind Robertson and Steele's excerpt from their book, subtitled "An Indictment of Formal Education, A Manifesto of Student Liberation." But I read a lot of truth here. I also read a recognition that we've built into education a cycle of whole audiences not caring or interdepending because they perceive non-caring in other audiences. Someone has to care, *say so,* and *act so,* to break into the cycle. Immense caring potential exists among students, faculty, and administrators, far in excess of the current motivation or opportunity to express it.

Problems of motivation and opportunity go beyond a simple recognition that campuses are systems of interdependent persons. We must ask, what kinds of systems are they? How can we build into them a sense of cooperative caring which could break the cycle of suspicion? Toward that end, I suggest you consider two ideas which have received quite a bit of attention in recent years, synergy and ecology.

Synergy

I understand the word "synergy" in two different ways. R. Buckminster Fuller in his speeches and books has explained well the relatively value-free and descriptive sense of the word. Any system viewed holistically has some form of cooperative, interactive potential different from

---

[2] Don Robertson and Marion Steele, *The Halls of Yearning: An Indictment of Formal Education, A Manifesto of Student Liberation* (S. F.: Canfield Colophon Books, 1969), p. 77.

76

ecology of academic audiences

what might be predicted from a simple observation of the separate parts of the system.[3] A system is more than the sum of its parts; it becomes a new entity, capable of new applications and inventiveness, and in the case of learning systems, new ways of caring and cooperation. Small groups engaged in decision-making often find an X-factor at work wherein interaction exploring various alternatives, sometimes even weird or silly ones, can produce a creative solution seemingly beyond the potential of individual members.

Fulfillment of capability isn't guaranteed; only capability. I'm thinking now of my frustration in a group the other day in which we let ourselves be paralyzed by each other. The decision confronting us could very well have been handled individually by any of us, I suspect. But we agreed to try to do it as a group. Role problems interfered; I was on edge because I felt the others were expecting me to lead the group. They were on edge, I believe, because they were afraid I was there less as a participant than as a judge. Silence. Half-hearted comments. Jittery talk about our jitters.

Synergy was still at work, but not a positive, energizing synergy. We *didn't* learn together as much as we *could* have learned alone. But we *could* have learned more together, unpredictably more, if our communication assumptions had been different. Synergy is basically a communication concept, and is positively valued to the extent that our interaction is satisfying and connected.

Anthropologist Ruth Benedict and humanistic psychologist Abraham Maslow use "synergy" as a term with positive connotation in its own right. Drawing on Benedict's research, Maslow distinguishes between high-synergy and low-synergy relationships.[4] High-synergy conditions encourage individual actions which are at the same time helpful to the actor and the social system. High-synergy suggests your advantages are my advantages; your gain is not my loss. We cooperate in sharing goals and the system we constitute is strengthened. Low-synergy systems, though, encourage competitive, win-lose confrontations. Power is at a premium, and you and I as participants are constantly checking to see whether our status measures up. Have to keep up with Jones. His *A* in organic chemistry may be the last squeeze on you, assuring him a place in med school, you a place as a supermarket checker. You both know Professor Y has only so many *A's* to give.

Students and teachers act as though there is a highly restricted quantity of reward-for-learning available and that students barter learn-

---

[3] *See* R. Buckminster Fuller, *Operating Manual for Spaceship Earth* (N. Y.: Pocket Books, 1970).

[4] Abraham H. Maslow, *The Farther Reaches of Human Nature* (N. Y.: Viking Press, 1971), pp. 199-211.

students as real people

ing for reward. Learning is not the reward in this system, it is the work done *for the reward*. Students are workers.

The questions of what-will-be-taught-and-how are decided by the foremen (the faculty) in close cooperation with the management (the administration) which is, of course, appointed by the board of trustees (the absentee owners of the factory).[5]

James Weaver further observes quite sardonically:
The education factory of the twentieth century is less physiologically damaging than were the factories of the nineteenth century, and for that we can be thankful. None of today's students are dying from lockjaw as the result of phosphorus in the air. The psychological damage, however, is about the same.[6]

Weaver's analogy suggests the destructiveness of low-synergy assumptions in campus life. Then we expect students to transcend the assumptions and love learning for its own sake. Faculty wonder why student groups so seldom cooperate with us, why bright students often disdain formal channels of university governance, why we are made fun of in barely disguised ways.

I'm optimistic about change, but I don't look for administration to try to increase the synergy of the college campus. It's concerned with economics, maintenance, organization, and generally avoiding crises. All such things are important and influence learning and interaction climates, but are unlikely to alter them greatly. The inertia of the status quo is great indeed.

Although faculties should be close to student needs, don't look for too much help from us, either. Goodstein's research shows:

Many, if not most, faculty people have little or no interest or concern with educational objectives, either with those of their particular institution or those of general education. They see themselves as narrow subject-matter specialists, concerned with their advancement of and in their respective academic disciplines. They seem far more interested in transmitting subject matter than in changing values and attitudes, and it is not surprising that student attitudes and values do not get changed.[7]

---

[5] James H. Weaver, "The Student as Worker," *The University and Revolution*, ed. Gary R. Weaver and James H. Weaver (Englewood Cliffs, N. J.: Prentice-Hall, 1969), p. 63.

[6] Ibid., p. 65

[7] Leonard Goodstein, "Institutional Research on Students: A Summing up," *Research on College Students*, ed. Hall T. Sprague (Boulder: The Western Interstate Commission for Higher Education, 1960), p. 129.

ecology of academic audiences

This faculty ethic is a sad but persistent feature of college life, though I believe I'm seeing more receptivity to student needs among today's teachers. One part of Goodstein's comment is particularly disagreeable to me, though I am generally sympathetic to his idea. I've never felt good about teachers who try to "change" student values and attitudes; that's hardly the opposite of "transmitting subject matter," hardly an implementation of the synergic assumption.

Ecology

Lee Thayer, writing of alternative approaches to the theory of communication, has suggested that "normal human environments" can be classified as either "physical environments" directly ascertainable by our senses, or "communicational environments" composed of the ways we talk about our experience. Each system maintains its own ecology, or relationship-balance, with the communicational system ". . .having existence only in and through the fact of its talk-about-ableness."[8]

Thayer's approach reminds me of an essay by novelist/ecologist Edward Hyams in which a distinction is drawn between two broad classes of tools. Physical tools (usually the only ones people tend to think of as "tools") allow us to act directly with the world, altering its physical appearance in some way. Though psychological tools are more easily expressed in methods or techniques, "philosophically, there is no difference between these two classes of tools: the plan a man makes concerning the way in which he will move a boulder, is just as much a tool as the lever he uses to carry out his plan."[9] Psychological tools, in this sense, are useful in shaping Thayer's communicational environment, not only if they stress overt method and data (a subdivision Hyams labels "intellectual tools"), but also because they stress "whys" and relationships ("spiritual tools").

You and I act purposefully in (on) our physical and communicational worlds by alerting ourselves to their respective ecologies, accepting them on their own terms, and then applying only those tools of change which respect the integrity of what is there.

An ecological approach offers a way of recognizing and organizing my life choices that is both exciting and appealing. My potential, even survival, is bounded by the flexibility of the environment which sustains me. When it becomes inflexible, I am cornered. I microcosm environment; environment is an extension of me. It is not useful to distinguish

---

[8] Lee Thayer, "Human Communication: Tool, Game, Ecology," *Perspectives on Communication,* ed. Carl E. Larson and Frank E. X. Dance (Milwaukee: University of Wisconsin—Milwaukee Speech Communication Center, 1968), p. 17.

[9] Edward Hyams, "Tools of the Spirit," *Sources,* ed. Theodore Roszak (N. Y.: Harper Colophon Books, 1972), p. 328.

students as real people

between poisoning the air and poisoning me; I breathe. Do you DDT crops? You DDT me; I eat. I'm becoming increasingly, if belatedly, aware of my responsibility to decide when I'm strengthening the resource patterns of my environment, when I'm depleting them, and when I'm polluting them. Civilization will eventually become fully aware that it can't encourage unrestrained consumption. Consumption depletes. Cyclic usage patterns make the only kind of good sense when quantities seem finite but wants do not. Flexibility, balance, and relationship become the key concepts, key tools. We're all in this together, I'm told by a television ad.

Ironically, students generally have been very vocal in their support of sane ecological policies in the physical environment, and almost completely neglectful of these same concerns in their own most immediate communication environment, the campus interaction system. Granted, as Mark Terry puts it, "Our conventions and habits of communication have come to make certain environmental relationships difficult to express and hence easy to overlook."[10] You may have noticed I'm grappling with some unconventional and fairly rag-tag language in describing ecology. (Our language seems to encourage the description of things, not processes or interrelationships.) But students on the whole have been able to respond meaningfully to "save our environment" pleas. Many of you have marched, petitioned, boycotted, and voted as you have because you've seen clearly that "we're all in this together," that everything is related to everything else.

Thayer reminds us that the same attitude must apply to any group of people. Each group develops its own form of ecological balance which must be taken into account. The campus environment can be improved by addressing the very same ecological questions which apply to the physical environment. I see those questions as:

(1) What and where are the available resources?
(2) In what ways do the resources interrelate and interdepend?
(3) What are the available supplies and our needs for them?
(4) What are the dangerous pollutants? Necessary ones?
(5) How can we best implement recycling networks?
(6) How do we juggle answers to questions 1-5 to achieve a livable, workable, balance?

If you think of learning as the best, most satisfying outcome of your college experience, you can think of yourself as a chooser. You can think further of your transactions with other choosers as the chief determi-

---

[10] Mark Terry, *Teaching for Survival* (N.Y.: Ballantine Books, 1971), p. 143.

80

ecology of academic audiences

nants of your learning. You can think of the communication ecology of personal student choice.

What and Where Are the Available Resources?

Thinking of only the physical learning environment of higher education might encourage you to identify books, films, lecture notes, libraries, language laboratories, theaters, pens, tape recorders, No-Doze, and the like as your prime resources. I guess most are pretty important. Most of them probably even relate closely to your communication habits. Maybe you could identify money as a root-resource, since enough of it can insure the secondary resources. Unfortunately, since the richest people (and colleges) in my experience are often not the wisest, my persistent suspicion is that learning depends upon an interrelated but largely different set of assumptions.

Resources are actually assumptions. Often we have discovered by serendipity or sweat a new use for a particular pattern of matter/energy which transformed it *by definition* into a resource. We did it with coal, uranium, and orange juice. Our assumptions about matter/energy's usableness and usefulness determine whether we use the label "resource."

Consider this statement from one of the leading analysts of behavior in our time, anthropologist Gregory Bateson:

Social flexibility is a resource as precious as oil or titanium and must be budgeted in appropriate ways, to be spent (like fat) upon needed change. . . .Flexibility may be defined as uncommitted potentiality for change.[11]

Bateson's distinction, consistent with those of Thayer and Hyams, invites you to consider how much flexibility prevails on your campus. Beware, you may have a hard time seeing flexibility if you feel no power to act meaningfully to affect the system. Often, students never discover how flexible a teacher might be in reconsidering a grade simply because they never inquire, assert their disagreement, or explain their behavior fully.

Perhaps flexibility is a root-resource in our communication environment analagous to money in the physical realm. If so, it's ironic that people often tend to deny their own flexibility by saying "I can't" when they mean "I won't" or "I choose not to" or "it's inconvenient for me." It's tough to realize that you contain your own best potential resources, but you need to choose to commit them for purposes of self-change.

Giving direction to your communication flexibility can be the role of some additional resources. For example, your opinions—expressions

---

[11] Gregory Bateson, *Steps to an Ecology of Mind* (N. Y.: Ballantine Books, 1972), p. 497.

students as real people

of attitudes—can serve as valuable resources for your own (and others') education. You learn about yourself by hearing yourself talk, by paying attention to how you attempt to clarify your inner meaning so that it may be understood by another. During this process of word selection, you compare, contrast, interplay ideas one against the other. I've sometimes doubted I had a hold on a difficult concept until I self-examined myself in process by telling a friend, noticing myself surprising myself by the ease with which the verbal symbols seemed to connect with and specify the previously vague notion. One of my favorite books written for the beginning speech student is Brown and Van Riper's *Speech and Man*. The authors appear to be talking about the same resource when they describe a "directioning tendency" which provides momentum for speech which in turn clarifies and informs thought:

> Over and over again, when we have asked students why they enrolled in our course in speech they have answered, "I want to learn to be able to think on my feet." What they mean is that they wish to be able to start with a dim, embryonic hunch of a thought and to help it emerge, one appropriate word following another until, lo! the formulation is complete and adequate. They want to be able to think aloud with ease. They know of course that none of us, except in special circumstances, ever rehearses word for word a thought which is to be expressed. We begin with a felt need to say something. We dimly know what we want to say, but the actual verbal programming takes place only after we start moving our mouths.[12]

Brown and Van Riper suggest that the importance of such verbal explanation/exploration is one of the bases of creativity, for what happens in thought is often the mere " . . . sketching the outlines of the pattern that could only get completed by the utterance itself."[13]

I believe this is why it was usually easier for me to study with another concerned student in the same course than to study alone. It could explain, too, that upsetting experience of getting exciting ideas in conversations (when I can't write them down expediently) rather than when I'm cloistered in my office with reams of frustratingly blank paper. Perhaps our study habits could stand some scrutiny in light of what we know about communication, creativity, and ecology.

Examine your campus experience to determine how often you're expected to have a voice, though. To the extent that you are not given or do not take opportunities to talk in your education, you are being

---

[12] Charles T. Brown and Charles Van Riper, *Speech and Man* (Englewood Cliffs, N. J.: Prentice-Hall, 1966), pp. 102-103.

[13] Ibid., p. 103.

82

ecology of academic audiences

robbed of self-discovery learning. More obviously, to the extent that other students do not talk, you are robbed further. Communication resources are wasted when they are usable, useful, and unused, because time is a resource, too.

I could highlight numerous other factors I consider resources in the communication environment of higher education—cooperation, acceptance, trust, caring, etc. I've written of these earlier in other ways. But I think you've glimpsed my idea by now; I've already run the danger of belaboring the obvious. But it's disturbing sometimes how disguised the obvious can get if we don't talk about it every now and then.

In What Ways Do the Resources Interdepend?

As in the physical environment, the key to the ecology of the educational communication environment is interdependence. Human encounters, even momentary ones, have communication consequences that go far beyond the experience of the participants. Perhaps this reassures; perhaps it disturbs.

Clearly, when you enter my office for our appointment, how we influence and understand each other is in part determined by the exam I just graded, my unsettling phone call from home, and my worry about my grandmother who is ill. Less clear, but no less real, are such factors as the teacher I encountered long ago who convinced me that education was a worthy profession, the quality and goals of my parents' relationship before I was born, and my choice to take this job instead of the other one I was offered five years ago. Most if not all of these factors remain mysteries to you, lurking ghosts influencing you in subtle and significant ways. You bring ghosts, too, through which I am changed. Humans are inevitably jostled by the ripples emanating from unseen and unconsidered acts. We live in a world in which everything appears to affect everything else. Ray Bradbury's short story "A Sound of Thunder" points to this, as does John Hartford's clever song, "I Would Not Be Here."[14]

The same interdependence applies to education generally. The effectiveness of your ability to talk in education (resource: whether you have a *voice*) largely depends upon whether you perceive yourself as possessing communicational flexibility (resource: whether you have a *choice*). And vice-versa. My dividing the discussion earlier into two parts was artificial indeed. Actually, any question of boundaries, walls, labels, and limits when referring to systems will inevitably seem somewhat artificial. But especially here, the two concerns of voice and choice weave in and out of each other incessantly in student behavior:

---

[14] Ray Bradbury, *R is for Rocket* (N. Y.: Doubleday, 1962); John Hartford's song is from the RCA album "Gentle On My Mind and Other Originals," LSP-4068.

students as real people

"I can't talk with Dr. Smith. He's so intelligent, he makes me feel insignificant." (lack of choice→lack of voice)

"I tried to ask a question once in lecture. She made fun of me. I'll never ask another one." (lack of voice→lack of choice)

"Students will never be able to get anything done around here. Why run for student government?" (lack of choice→lack of voice)

"Yeah, I tried to write my own opinion once on a test. What a laugh! He only wanted his own answer rephrased. What's the use?" (lack of voice→lack of choice)

My characterizations in parentheses are open to dispute and highly tentative. Different interpretations are certainly possible. My main question, though, is simply this: don't these laments sound familiar? Granted, they characterize most human relationships at least occasionally; but their repetition in student union cafeterias at schools I've attended has reached near-ceremonial proportions.

Perceived flexibility and verbalization depend upon each other in giving a person a sense of competence in his or her environment. The other resources I've mentioned (cooperation, acceptance, trust, and caring) also interdepend and have been discussed in other chapters. Flexibility and informed choice thrive in high-synergy, noncompetitive, nonjudgmental atmospheres, as the literature on "brainstorming" illustrates,[15] while people tend to feel more comfortable speaking and inquiring in a supportive, accepting atmosphere than in an untrusting, evaluative, uncaring one.[16] Recounting the communication resource factors, in fact, creates nothing less than a criteria checklist for any strong and growing relationship.

What Are the Available Supplies and Our Needs For Them?

I believe that a person builds an education rather than receiving one. Building an education, like building a car, an auditorium, or a city, takes resources. Our civilization's needs (or greeds, as the case may be) have often been met by policies which seriously deplete our resources of timberland, oil, fresh water, and the like. That doesn't have to happen.

---

[15] Alex F. Osborn, *Applied Imagination: Principles and Procedures of Creative Thinking* (rev. ed.; N. Y.: Charles Scribner's Sons, 1957).

[16] Jack R. Gibb, "Defensive Communication," *The Journal of Communication*, 11 (September, 1961), 141-148.

ecology of academic audiences

American culture has led itself to a blind acceptance of what sociologist Philip Slater has called the "scarcity assumption."[17] Quantities of resources are limited, the claim goes, thus there are not enough rewards to go around, and each of us must compete with others incessantly to insure that we get our fair share. To Slater, the scarcity assumption is the organizing mythology of the "old culture," whether one talks of physical or communicational resources. In fact, resources are plentiful enough to go around, if ecological cooperation is encouraged. The competition developed out of our anxious user-ism strains the communication environment far beyond its credible flexibility.

The communication environment especially lends itself to the perception of resources in qualitative terms rather than quantitative. Once we begin to perceive in this new way, personal and interpersonal resources like voice, choice, cooperation, acceptance, trust, and caring become obvious while institutionally defined pseudo-resources like grades, scholarships, campus government power, student work clout, and the like become exposed for what they are—at best, partial means to ill-defined ends for a few elite students. And while some of these means may be in artificially short supply—teachers may "curve" their grades to limit the number of A's—the truer, more basic communicational resources are in unlimited supply. We have only to recognize our desperate need for them.

I am aware that such suggestions might be criticized as unrealistic. I am aware that some of my colleagues in higher education believe such a view is hopelessly naive and pollyanna-ish, that educational resources will always have to be based on money, power, grades, threats, and status differences. But occasionally I'm encouraged by what appears to be the tip of the iceberg of change. More and more, educators are noticing:

> Students are pitted against one another in competition for scarce resources in the form of high grades. Since grades must be allocated on the basis of "objective" and therefore standardized criteria, representations of personal or idiosyncratic creativity receive little encouragement. The student learns that while short-term success—such as a good first job, quality graduate school, financial support—is highly dependent on good grades, they may not be indicators of long-term success. The good student, even more than others, resents a society that places a high value on a narrow criterion. He finds that his self-esteem suffers under such an idea. . . .[18]

---

[17] Philip Slater, *The Pursuit of Loneliness: American Culture at the Breaking Point* (Boston: Beacon Press, 1970), Chapter 5.

[18] Irving Louis Horowitz and William H. Friedland, *The Knowledge Factory: Student Power and Academic Politics in America* (Carbondale: Southern Illinois University Press Arcturus Books, 1972), p. 133.

students as real people

But most attempts to reduce the system's reliance on artificial resources (which are in short supply) in favor of more basic personal and interpersonal resources (which are limitless once we assume their possibility) are dismissed as permissiveness. Permissiveness is a dirty word to many, symbolic of a form of "child-raising" which doesn't "care enough" to discipline the child. Ex-college president Harold Taylor replies however that, to him, "permissiveness" in education truly means "gentleness, affection, openness, freedom, concern, honesty, and a willingness to permit others to act as they are. . . ."[19] He has glimpsed the possibility.

What Are the Environmental Pollutants?

I don't know about your yard, but in mine "weeds" are those plants which grow where I don't want them to, whatever the beauty or strength of the plant. I don't know about your ears, but to mine "noise" is any sound which interferes with what I want to hear at the time, whatever the beauty or melody of the sound. A rose can be a weed, Beethoven's Ninth a sequence of noises. In much the same way, "pollutant" can be defined as anything you have to expend resources to counteract. The matter is situational, as we are constantly reminded when, in an age of oil shortages, we are challenged by a series of oceanic oil spills which are ecologically destructive and very expensive to combat. One moment oil is resource; the next, pollutant.

Inappropriate application or placement makes any valuable resource a pollutant. Having a voice—feeling free to express yourself—is important, but speaking irresponsibly from a position of "voice" pollutes the rhetorical environment. Choice and flexibility are beneficial, too, but few things can be more frustrating to students than the "radical" teacher who is convinced he or she is reforming the system by telling students at the beginning of the term, "I respect your right to determine your own education. This is a speech class (or sociology, or literature. . .); what do you want to study and how?" Overchoice without guidelines pollutes. I believe it's a prime malady of the American experience a bit analagous to my own experience of finding a record sale where I could afford one or two albums. But there were so many I'd liked that the whole situation got out of hand and became so anxious for me that I retreated in futility, silence, and inner anger at my own lack of discipline. The teacher who builds overchoice into the classroom risks a similar reaction from students, many of whom want to learn as badly as I wanted to hear new music, but for whom the total lack of structure became disabling.

So, voice and choice may be pollutants, as well as crucial resources, and, though negative meanings and effects are often attributed to apathy, suspicion, fear, and even judgment, leading me sometimes to gener-

---

[19] Harold Taylor, *Students Without Teachers: The Crisis in the University* (N. Y.: McGraw-Hill, 1969), p. 220.

ecology of academic audiences

alize about their polluting nature, they too have other faces, other situations in which they could be justifiable.

How Can We Best Implement Recycling Networks?

Resources, if they are to be valuable to us, must be shared, and shared efficiently. They must be used again and again. They must be applied in as many different contexts of a human system as possible, profiting as many different audiences as possible. A resource used only once—or used by only one audience—creates a drag on the system.

I strongly believe we can recycle campus resources only by recognizing the common stake all audiences have in the resources. Thus, I am led to the final question. . .

How Do We Achieve a Livable, Workable Balance?

An entire volume could be written on an ecology of educational communication, while I've summarized the problem in a fraction of a chapter. That's dangerous in a way, but necessary in a way, too. The danger of course is oversimplification, but the necessity consists of relating the concept of ecology to the variety of academic audiences. I want to express as clearly as possible my belief that unless we approach the campus interaction system holistically as a growing, flexible unit with interdependent, intercommunicating subsystems, we will be doomed to constantly competitive relationships among the major academic audiences of student, faculty, and administration. These three main audiences often have such different values, needs, and assumptions about campus goals that cooperation for flexibility and open communication seems impossible. It's not, but believing it so immobilizes us.

I hope the remainder of this chapter, and more specifically, the next, will suggest some ways for us to alter this dangerous definition of our situation, producing the balance we need so desperately to learn.

You as Teachers' Audience, Teachers as Your Audience

No one can presume to tell you who you are, to define you for you. In this section, I don't mean to define you or your characteristics as much as I mean to share with you some generalized faculty perceptions of the student as a social type. If some of those characteristics seem to fit, fine. If they don't, then we have another example of your uniqueness, and that's fine, too.

If it is true that how teachers perceive students will determine how they will attempt to communicate with them, and this can hardly be doubted, then prospective students might prepare for barren times in-

students as real people

deed. Evidence, personal and public, suggests that too many college and university faculty see, or try to see, students as essentially similar, lower-order creatures who potentially stand in the way of promotions, tenure, and the real business of higher education, Research.

(I'm pretty uncomfortable with the generalization of the preceding paragraph. It's a conclusion I reach very reluctantly with full recognition of the numerous exceptions. I daily come into contact with teachers whose energy is committed to understanding and responding to the needs of students. An interesting thing about college life, though, is that almost all teachers wish to be characterized in this way (I just realized I'm no exception). An early idea in Ursula LeGuin's popular science fiction novel *The Left Hand of Darkness* is that no one considers himself or herself a traitor; "traitor" is other-accusation, not self-accusation or one's own image.[20] Similarly, "you're not enough concerned with students" is very rarely a self-accusation.)

I find it disturbing when Kenneth Keniston, one of our leading psychologists, can write that ". . . despite years of systematic research using students as subjects, there is astonishingly little knowledge of students as people."[21] Disturbing, but not surprising. Goodstein notes that ". . .there are almost no institutional rewards, with one or two exceptions, for faculty people who are interested in student attitudes and values. . . ."[22] No wonder many reach the easy conclusion that all students are pretty much alike, that students are by and large cut from the same cloth.[23]

Some faculty research, though, does distinguish types of students based upon student "subcultures." Clark and Trow have produced the most influential typology in their division of student culture into groups labeled "academic," "vocational," "collegiate," and "non-conformist."[24] Basically, "academics" study a lot and value grades highly. "Vocational" students see college as a specialized training ground for a specific future occupation. The "collegiate" subculture most values the social aspects of college life—fraternities, sororities, mixing at dances and parties. And finally, the "non-conformist" category includes a variety of activists and dissidents who do not fit easily into other categories.

The Clark and Trow system does make distinctions among students with different motivations, but the criterion for typing, based as it

---

[20] Ursula K. LeGuin, *The Left Hand of Darkness* (N. Y.: Ace, 1969), p. 42.

[21] Kenneth Keniston, "The Faces in the Lecture Room," *The Contemporary University: U.S.A.*, ed., Robert S. Morison (Boston: Houghton Mifflin, 1966), p. 316.

[22] Goodstein, p. 129.

[23] Paul Heist and Harold Webster, "Differential Characteristics of Student Bodies—Implications for Selection and Study of Undergraduates," *Selection and Educational Differentiation: Proceedings* (Berkeley: The Center for the Study of Higher Education, 1960).

ecology of academic audiences

is wholly on student commitment to ideas and the institution of college, is somewhat artificial and static. It seems to typologize student goals, but hardly gets to the issue of subculture, which is necessarily a communicative process. Sandeen believes:

> . . .this form of description alone remains inadequate in any serious attempt to understand student life on the campus, and its subsequent effect on the learning environment. One needs to probe carefully into the amount and kinds of interaction that occur among the various groups.[25]

In other words, if those students labeled "academic" tend not to interact with each other, creating their own system of well-defined norms, there may be academic tendencies on a particular campus, but calling that a "subculture" creates a misnomer at best. A subculture interacts, it is movement and process; and, as usual in the academic world, we have confused process with content—forcing active processes into static content molds.

The academic world has been unresponsive to Sandeen's call for a typology based on communication patterns. To me, the reason is pretty clear. If we started researching students as communicators, we might have to start facing the implications of viewing students as real people.

Teachers may see you as contents of a test tube, alike and as appealing as vials of hydrochloric acid, unmotivated, isolated, interruptions in the flow of the day. Not all do, but enough to stimulate intense resentment in the teacher[26] and despair in the sensitive student.

Of course, to the extent that you respond only as reactor—as expected—to your environment, letting outer definitions become inner, you *are* all those things. Unfree, unmotivated, uneducated. Dahms, in reporting the disturbing results of a research study at a large midwestern university, shows that education students need to be told what to do *more* as they stay in school *longer*. Thirty-seven per cent of juniors in this study had strong needs to be told what to do, while the figure rose to 44% of the seniors and 69% of the graduate students.[27]

But to the extent you see yourself as a unique individual who can share that uniqueness through significant interaction in subcultural

---

[24] Burton R. Clark and Martin Trow, "The Organizational Context," *College Peer Groups*, ed. Theodore M. Newcomb and Everett K. Wilson (Chicago: Aldine, 1966), pp. 17–70.

[25] Arthur Sandeen, "Communication Among Students," *Journal of Higher Education*, XXXIX (December, 1968), p. 513.

[26] Robertson and Steele, p. 22; Paul Goodman, *Compulsory Mis-education and The Community of Scholars* (N. Y.: Vintage Books, 1964), p. 267.

[27] Alan M. Dahms, *Emotional Intimacy: Overlooked Requirement for Survival* (Boulder: Pruett, 1972), p. 111.

students as real people

groupings and define self-proactively, you are not atomized, alike, experimentable, distasteful interruptions to teachers. You are what we need to survive sanely in the often barren academic world—responders, interdependent partners in the ecology of dialogue.

This ecology is continually threatened by a cycle of negative self-fulfilling expectations, a ferris wheel in search of a control. If I assume you're basically unmotivated, dishonest, and undisciplined, you'll notice all the controls I build into my class to make sure you will turn in papers on time, will not be able to cheat on exams, and will attend class sessions. There's a good chance you'll resent these controls which treat you like a child (though you may expect them and think you "need" them), and, in resenting them, will respond with rote acquiescence (most common), hostility, circumvention (looking for loopholes, cheating), or simply by overlooking them. Of course, most teachers only attend their *own* classes and come into contact with students who are responding to that one teacher and his or her courses. Not surprisingly, then, the teacher with negative expectations generalizes that students are basically unmotivated, dishonest if unguarded, and undisciplined. For this teacher, students *are* these things. The teacher searches regularly for innovative controls to make sure students sit still long enough to receive the unwanted but necessary inoculation of knowledge.

Faculty creativity is channeled into disciplining you rather than teaching/learning with you; your creativity is channeled into circumventing or ignoring imposed discipline rather than on teaching/learning with faculty.

In the past several years I've become convinced that many college professors are sincerely attempting to make their classrooms into effective learning centers, but are hampered by the walls which separate students from them. College teachers seem to me to fit within one of these descriptions: (1) they teach because they enjoy it, (2) they teach because they used to enjoy it and would like to again, or (3) they teach because they thought they'd enjoy it, never have, and would like to find a way. All three groups are potentially valuable allies for students in search of a meaningful learning community. Few if any teachers set out to dehumanize; most (I include myself here) just grope from approach to approach searching for a way to make a more meaningful difference on campus. The only way to do this seems to me to involve increased informal contact with students in and out of the classroom. But not long ago, the "Faculty Forum" on my campus, a periodical newsletter of faculty in-house opinion, carried an article by a professor who contended that faculty will not regain respect or increase salaries to compare with other professional groups until we reverse the trend toward informality—demonstrated, for instance, by students dropping the "Dr." from salutations to Ph.D. faculty. I don't wonder at the author's motives,

ecology of academic audiences

only his priorities. Recalling my student days, I realize I respected only persons, not titles.

It's difficult to teach. This is a fact contrary to some public images and a fact students could realize more often. Because if you know that, you begin to consider the hours spent late at night planning the lectures students make fun of. And if you know that, you begin to recognize the dilemmas of a professor whose value to the university is not measured in terms of how much time and energy he or she commits to you, but in how many articles are published in obscure scholarly journals. And if you know that, you begin to understand the private hours of dis-ease induced by trying to live (and administer) humanely under an often stifling and overcompetitive grading system. And you might begin to empathize with the late-at-night red-eyed lonely headaches from poring over term papers when there are two committees to prepare for by tomorrow morning. And you might begin to consider the stage fright of a man or woman to whom you've assigned the whole responsibility for making the class "work" for 15, 30, 50, 150, or sometimes even 500 divergent souls. Or the ego-shattering embarrassment of not knowing the obvious answer to a second row question. Or the sinking feeling that a whole discussion group doesn't give a damn about the subject the teacher is so excited about, and the agonizing silence that dares him or her to deliver a monologue instead. Or the intense disappointment after asking an entire class to take home their anonymous course evaluations so they could spend more time responding to the value (or lack of it) of the course, and receiving none back.

Please consider too that these are not hypothetical examples.

Perhaps I'm prejudiced, but one thing is much clearer to me now than it was in my student days. Faculty people often desperately want to improve communication with students but either feel it is impossible or are consistently frustrated in their attempts to do so by student expectations of noninteraction, their own denial of the resource of flexibility, or by bureaucratic structure. What we need—what I need—is some response from you with which we may modify future behavior to facilitate understanding.

The Future of an Ecology of Audiences

Obviously, since I continue to return to this idea, since all my separate departures-of-idea eventually converge toward it, I believe that the key to organizing a healthy campus ecology lies in making the student/faculty communication link more tangible, permanent, and empathic. Just as species cannot change abruptly except with rare and disturbing mutations, so must bureaucracies and their rules change by evolution. No purely administrative change or set of changes will make a

students as real people

dent in the ecological problems of the campus. Strengthening student governments alone won't do it, nor will electing students to Boards of Trustees or university budget committees, forming more student pressure groups, or hiring an "understanding" president. "Even in the largest universities, what it finally comes down to is one student and one teacher, no matter how many others are in the community surrounding both persons."[28] Nothing will really improve until students and faculty clarify the real interpersonal purposes behind our relationship. Erich Fromm belives this can be done if teachers

> . . . cease being bureaucrats hiding their own lack of aliveness behind their role of bureaucratic dispensers of knowledge; if they become—in a word, by Tolstoy—"the codisciples of their students."[29]

Teachers may have to make that first excursion into the cycle of negative expectations I explained earlier. But this is my affirmation and plea to you: individual students are important; you can help, you can facilitate, you can encourage, you can allow this to happen. Perhaps by your skillful allowing, you can make the change inevitable.

---

[28] Taylor, p. 183.

[29] Erich Fromm, *The Revolution of Hope: Toward a Humanized Technology* (N.Y.: Bantam, 1968).

7

action, reaction, and inaction in higher education

We have no maps for a lot of the new territory we are entering, but we have good humor and courage and imagination. It is true space exploration. Inner space as well as outer. It takes courage from all of us, teachers/students/administrators, to work together toward the future. We may well ask ourselves what equipment we need. We ask the questions and grow to the answers. We are exploring the new terrain, in our time, of a revolution in values, a new human consciousness and social order. Does somebody prefer the hazards of moon travel? I don't blame him.

M. C. Richards
The Crossing Point[1]

Dear Student...

I'd like to emphasize again why I'm writing these chapters more or less informally, as I would a letter. (Maybe this is your first letter complete with footnotes!) Letters are very unusual documents in the life of institutional education; the rhetoric of essay tests, term papers, memos, and textbooks is much more common. Letters are personal. Sometimes frivolous, sometimes serious. Letters are kind of spontaneous. Letters are what you write to friends, or, at least to people you feel strongly about. Letters, in other words, usually presume strong feeling, caring, and a specific desire to share with an identified audience. I write letters expecting they'll be read, and carefully. I watch my mailbox with anticipation, hoping to receive the letters of others and give them that same attention.

---

[1] M. C. Richards, *The Crossing Point: Selected Talks and Writings* (Middletown, Conn.: Wesleyan University Press, 1973), p. 111.

students as real people

I like the style and "feel" of letters, but my out-of-town friends could tell you that it is somewhat rare for me to motivate myself to write. They get no avalanche of letters from me because I tend to write only when it feels important, only when consequences seem immediate.

That's why I'm addressing you now through an extended letter style. The more traditional "scholarly" writing style stresses objectivity and detachment, and I'm basically uncomfortable with it. Certainly it is even more uncomfortable when I feel a subject and a concern passionately. What I have to say here is important, and the consequences are immediate, for you and for me. As you have probably observed, the thing which almost constantly troubles me about American education is that students are neither allowed nor, often, seem to want the choices of *persons* interacting with other *persons* in building an education that matters. I simply want to reaffirm that you have the possibility of personal choice, a freedom of potential which directly counters the idea that college and university life is some sort of inexorable slow struggle, a Darwinian "survival of the fittest" situation to which "A" students have adapted themselves successfully often through monologue, and can react to mechanically in one dimension. Phillips, Butt, and Metzger's idea of the compliant student is one you might profit by considering at length:

> What most teachers do not understand is that the students who are present and obedient may also not be learning, they may only be complying. Much behavior that teachers evaluate positively and thus reward can be classified as "compliance behavior."
>
> 1. Compliance behavior is characterized by the ability of the student to pass the tests that teacher devises with high marks according to the teacher's evaluation. The compliant student will be equally adept at objective and essay type tests.
>
> 2. The compliant student will conform to the rules of the classroom. He will speak when he is invited, he will remain quiet when others are speaking. He will not violate school rules.
>
> 3. The compliant student will do things that please teacher and he will do them only for that purpose.
>
> 4. The compliant student will rarely threaten teacher with questions he cannot answer or with requests for help that he cannot fulfill.
>
> 5. The compliant student is generally neat and comes from a "good family."
>
> While it may seem cynical to say so, it is students who fit that description who receive the maximum rewards from the school system.[2]

---

[2] Gerald M. Phillips, David E. Butt, and Nancy J. Metzger, *Communication in Education: A Rhetoric of Schooling and Learning* (N. Y.: Holt, Rinehart and Winston, 1974), p. 102.

action, reaction, and inaction

Obviously I don't know whom to blame for this tendency. I do know it's not important for me to blame. Whom do I blame for evolutionary natural selection? Darwin? The Unseen Creator? Apes? Dinosaurs? The process just *is*, that's all.

Blame is reaction. I want to be able to act on my environment to change it—if I choose to—so that we may participate more fully together. Action is more vital to our well-being than mere reaction. I believe students fundamentally want to be able to act on their environment to change it, not react to an environment by letting it change them. If you decide to act to change the environment/assumptions of higher education, to emphasize interpersonal communication as learners, then natural selection and evolutionary change will still be at work, though the criteria will have certainly changed.

Doing

I just realized that I consistently ask in letters and phone calls what my friends "are doing" and that they almost always respond with activities not associated with school. Same with "how are you doing?" Could it be that we don't normally associate action—doing—with education at all? A frightening thought. Could it be that we have defined our educations as areas of life others wouldn't be interested in? Could it be we actually *aren't* doing anything in schools?

Therefore, my interest in you, and the reason I'm writing this letter. How are *you* doing? What are *you* doing?

If you should decide to make your education truly a communication experience, I believe you could recognize a wide range of choices for direct action. There are a lot of things you can *do* to implement this idea in your school relationships. Education is never just reaction. Education can never be inaction. True education is always action.

When I began to write this book, I didn't have in mind a "how to do it" or even a "what to do" manual. I saw more need for a "why it needs to be done" and a "why you can do it" approach. I still do; cookbooks are too plentiful and our ingredients too different. But I now see more clearly that I'd like to be specific about how you and I can act to introduce the resource of flexibility into this environment.

Action Alternatives

As a result of familiarizing yourself with concepts of humanistic interpersonal communication, you might begin to build a personal list of possibilities for you to act differently on campus. I encourage you to take responsibility only for your own list, and to build it carefully, taking into

students as real people

consideration your personality, value system, and the nature of your campus. Mine is very generalized and merely . . . mine.

I've placed in the left-hand column what could be called assumptive student behavior; institution and student alike assume or tend to assume these to be proper. For each, there appears a corresponding item in the right-hand column which hopefully will suggest an action alternative which could set up more possibilities for learning. Please realize that not all left-column items are untrue or undesirable, though they may be incomplete notions of what is possible. Not all right-column items should be considered substitutes for the assumptive behaviors, either. They may simply be supplementary to the other ideas, reminders that choices exist and combinations are probably infinite.

Higher Education Assumes Students Will or Should:	(process/skill)	You Also Have or Should Have the Option to:
1. learn in isolation	(community)	1. seek, recognize, and build community
2. communicate intellectually	(wholeness)	2. develop your ability to communicate on emotional levels
3. profit by learning to judge and persuade	(acceptance)	3. substitute description and statement skills for judgment and persuasion
4. go to class	(be-ing)	4. *be* in class
5. receive reasons	(reason-ing)	5. supply your own reasons
6. answer questions about lessons	(question-ing)	6. have questions and ask questions
7. be unconcerned with administrative details of the campus	(research)	7. investigate the system thoroughly

action, reaction, and inaction

| 8. not participate responsibly and effectively in governance | (governance) | 8. commit yourself responsively to campus decisioning processes |

It is unnecessary here to include much explanation of the current assumptions of higher education. I wrote at length about such expectations in Chapter 2 and have referred to them several times since. But not all the behavioral alternatives are self-evident or self-explanatory, so I'd like to comment briefly on each.

Option 1
Seek, Recognize, and Build Community

I find "community" a hard concept to define. It goes beyond ordinary connotations of "neighborhood" to point (for me) to a state of being. Community seems to be one of those interpersonal states which seems ephemeral and unnecessarily abstract when I'm not directly experiencing it, but utterly, simply, tangible when I am. Almost like: "How do I know if I'm in love?" "You're not." When I'm in-community, I know it; I know that it exists, and I can begin to isolate some factors which characterize the state. But to define it? I'd rather describe my experience and let you define it yourself.

For me, community experiences have tended to involve:

(1) some shared and affirming *reason* for why I'm with these others, plus—occasionally—an almost mystical sense of "this is right for me, right now, to be where I am"
(2) the noticing of individuals in the group as persons, not just members
(3) the relatively free expression of my individual wants and needs
(4) the right to divergence and mistakes while remaining accepted
(5) a self-evolved, self-maintaining structure appropriate to the group's requirements
(6) identification with the goals of the group/organism growing—I am "it," it is "me"

A lot of groups have provided me with these things—but only rarely have they involved institutional curricular education. Athletic teams provided a taste of the bolstering feelings associated with community, as did some other extra-curricular activities such as debating. Residential groupings on campuses provide strong possibilities for develop-

students as real people

ing community; I know I missed dormitory life after I left much more than I could have predicted (or admitted) before I moved out. But, regrettably, the Committee on the Student in Higher Education offers this commentary:

> The creation of communities which would presumably work together, study together, and play together may be of decisive importance, especially in the multiversity, in overcoming the alienation and frustration which are at the root of much student unrest. At least it ought to be possible to convert residence halls into places where small groups of students, with a handful of faculty members, could create a living, learning community. Within these smaller residence halls, which might still be part of much larger complexes, some classroom instruction could take place, there could be some common meals, and as much seminar discussion as possible. This kind of innovation ought to be relatively simple, but it is not likely to occur until there is a major shift in the values of the university, making the importance of this sort of innovation unquestioned. In the meantime, skyscraper dormitories, which would be appropriate as penal institutions but are hardly appropriate as educational houses, will continue to spring up.[3]

This idea of living-based learning communities might give you something to shoot for in the long run, some idea to suggest to the powers that be, but I'm realistic about it. Few of you will have that opportunity university-sanctioned. So, if you want it badly enough, you'll just have to organize yourselves into groups of sharers. This I've seen, and it works as a learning environment. A famous academician once noted such potential and remarked that if he were starting a university, he'd build dormitories first, then a student center. If money was left over, he'd build and stock a library. Finally would come the ultimate frill, a classroom building.

You can seek community in a lot of places—organized extra-curricular activities you enter, the place you reside, the political and social action groups you join. Your college education may be sadly incomplete without this kind of fulfilling interaction, but don't wait for the institution to encourage it. You'll wait a long time, and alone. You have to *seek* it, *recognize* it when you find it, and help to *build* it to be a more potent force after you affiliate. The skills of *Students as Real People*—self-awareness, listening, honest messages, and audience empathy—will undoubt-

---

[3] The Committee on the Student in Higher Education, *The Student in Higher Education* (New Haven, Conn.: The Committee on the Student in Higher Education, 1968), pp. 49-50.

action, reaction, and inaction

edly help, but despite the importance of community to education, educators will probably not be much help to you. Building community is at present almost wholly a student force.

Nowhere is this more evident than the everyday classroom. Obstacles to community in the classroom are too numerous to detail here, and probably too obvious. But community is possible, if students make it so. In classrooms you're more reliant on teachers' procedures and the nature of the subject. But if you see a way to implement community learning in a class, don't keep it secret; tell Professor Z that you believe (for example) that ongoing discussion groups might provide a worthwhile supplement to other activities. Maybe you'll want to go to Professor Z in a group which has already discussed *both* the "lesson" and the mechanics of organizing the group or groups. Let the mode of your request demonstrate the effectiveness of your request. Let your process and your content merge.

(Speaking of classroom communities, I've included in Appendix A and Appendix B letters I wrote to two classes, SPC 514 for graduate students and SPC 310 for undergraduates. Each was offered during a summer break session as an intensive forty-hour one week workshop, and each focused on interracial communication. All of us in the groups wrote ungraded letters instead of analytical term papers; letters to each other, the group, employers, or outside friends or relatives. No limitations were placed on content. I believe each letter indicates something of my feeling about community which arose out of that particular experience. They may not be what I'd write today on the subject to these same people, but I'm satisfied that the letters were true to what I meant then.)

I have witnessed several instances when my campus, Southern Illinois University at Edwardsville, began to take on a community *flavor* (though not all the characteristics of community) in spite of its basic commuter atomization. I want to share some of these. One was during the streaking craze of the spring of 1974 when various organizations vied with each other to stage the definitive group streak. Rumors flew concerning time schedules, evasive techniques, "parade routes," participants, and the degree of seriousness with which Campus Security was taking these shenanigans. Classes were cut wholesale in order for large crowds to gather at vaguely understood times in the central mall, hoping collectively that "it" would happen. At these times, suited faculty bumped into blue-jeaned students, who bumped into middle-aged civil service staff, who bumped into—really—smiling administrators. Clearly an important "it" was happening that went beyond those rare times bodies were ogled: there was a genuine dissolving of the stuffiness and division of campus subgroups. A common comic relief evolved, a common sense release of tension, a bit of slowly savored joy and rejuvena-

students as real people

tion that bound diverse people together and became more important than the usual "let's-get-on-with-it" attitude.

I treasured those days. Some, of course, thought streaking a waste of time. Letters to the editor inquired, "what did it prove?," and I had no answer. If they'd asked, "what did it allow?," I'd have had a very good answer indeed.

Other instances of community flavor have been occurring periodically on a smaller scale. Every so often, the University Center and the Communications Building vibrate with several hundred grade schoolers who come on campus to view a University Theater production of "Peter and the Wolf," "Mother Goose," or some such entertainment. It's difficult for students not to stop and notice the wonder and amazement the little strangers exhibit, and how quickly they cease being strangers. The little ones make friends fast with the college population, demonstrating something valuable to commuter students who often work hard to remain strangers to each other. Wonder and amazement, freely expressed, rub off. It's as simple as that. Small, transient, spontaneous, but real communities form around the kids. Maybe Jerry Farber was right when he suggested that one good and direct action to humanize campuses was for everyone to bring a child one day, or, if you couldn't find one, a water buffalo.[4]

There's a lesson to be learned about cooperation and learning in community; it cannot be rigidly constructed, and its outlines cannot be discerned in advance. Because of its commuter personality, SIUE often has a difficult time securing audiences for scheduled speakers and performers. Recently, activist lawyer William Kunstler was incensed that his appearance drew only thirty people, and a pair of Japanese students touring the country to debate American students on the topic of U. S. foreign policy attracted the same number—most of whom were from a class asked to attend. But when a student group brought to campus Stephen Baird, a Boston "street singer," and invited him to set up shop unannounced on the floor of the main classroom building lobby, magic began to happen, and many of us sat childlike, amazed and wondering at the scope of this man's education. Some didn't stop, and noticed only that stairwells were a bit clogged and harder to get to; others did stop and discovered a different kind of class to choose for that afternoon. Though there was a clearly focused performer, I was acutely aware of others in the audience and a common we-are-a-part-of-something-special feeling.

Another time, absolutely without announcement, Ken Feit, a traveling self-proclaimed "fool," sat cross-legged with a brown paper bag on the floor of the central lounge area of the University Center, and began to apply whiteface and don a gaudy outfit. "The fool" had a variety of

---

[4] Jerry Farber, *The Student as Nigger* (N. Y.: Pocket Books, 1970), p. 60.

action, reaction, and inaction

wondrous items in his bag—socks, a banana, a soap bubble pipe, a kernel of unpopped corn—which he silently, theatrically, and eloquently experienced nonverbally as if for the first time, as a child. And I was transported back again to when I was a child, and everyday items were mysteries to be solved, not tools of habit. He perceived these things new, fully, in all their potential, in all his potential. Perhaps two hundred of us gathered spontaneously there that day to learn a lesson in perception and awareness, to be entertained, and later to share our individual perceptions with those people standing nearby. It was the most attentive I've ever seen a group of that many people at a university; it beat any lecture hall. Onlookers I talked with felt they were a part of something very important and timeless. We were together, focusing on stimulus, experience, interexperience. Again, a transient but real community happened, only because its members allowed it, refusing to proclaim the easy indictment, "it can't work here."

By the way, I also overheard a comment from one student who had paused for a minute to see what the crowd was about: "This is dumb. I've got to get to class. See ya."

Option 2
Develop Your Ability to Communicate On Emotional Levels

Hypothetical: you and I are sitting in the cafeteria over coffee at the end of the term. You've just handed in your final paper to me for SPC 301, "Principles of Small Group Communication," and we are both in relaxed, talkative moods. "Well, now that it's over," I ask, "how do you feel about the course?"

What do you say?

Think about it.

Of course, I'd probably not actually ask that at such a time; wouldn't have the nerve. Defies protocol in many ways. But I know people who would ask it, and do.

Have you decided how you'd respond?

I observe that most people around colleges respond to "how do you feel about . . ." inquiries in one of three ways. First, many respond to it as if it were a time-filler or small talk, a meaningless bridge to more important topics. Responses in this vein: "okay" or "fine." I realize there's a chance you might answer me this way, since there's a power angle to our relationship whether we like it or not, and you might want to remain noncommital.

Second, many people treat "how do you feel about . . ." questions as requests for judgment or evaluation. Responses: "it was really good," "it was kind of slow," or "seemed to leave out a lot." Given our relationship, I'd guess some sort of mildly positive evaluation might be closer to your

101

students as real people

reply, even though *it does not answer my question.* I did not ask for a judgment of externals, but people often like to judge, and look for opportunities.

Third, partially because of this pervasive human temptation, we often hear "how do you feel about . . ." questions as preliminaries to persuasion, or the first subtle shots in a war of opinions. If you are afraid of losing such a war, or simply don't want to do battle, you could respond: "how do *you* feel about it?" (in other words, "you can't trick me—you commit yourself first, then maybe I will"), or "I dunno," or "why do you want to know?"

Few in education hear such inquiries as an invitation to report actual internal affective reaction, though that is literally what is being invited. Despite this problem, no question is more on the minds of teachers; no question is censored from their lips more often. I know the defensive pressure students feel to supply the "right" answer. Instead, if I could be sure we trusted each other in dialogue, and if you interpreted me appropriately literally, I could ask in conversation or written form that question, "how do you feel about the course?," and you might be free to respond: "I'm frightened by it most of all, confused and frightened." Or: "I am elated!" Or: "I'm sad it's ending and I won't see many of these people again." Or: "I felt hostility toward the grading system at first, but now I'm sure proud of my 'B'!"[5]

In fact, your habit of telling me your feelings might free me to inquire more easily and readily into them when it is important for me as a teacher to do so. Again, the amazement of dialogue lies in its *mutual* benefits, but often *unilateral* initiation.

Option 3
Substitute Description and Statement Skills for Judgment and Persuasion

Recently I asked a group to pair off and sit quietly facing each other for three minutes. The only other instruction was to look at the other person and notice as many things about them as possible. After the three minutes, each was to spend three to five minutes telling the other what was noticed. In the sharing of experiences when the large group reconvened, some interesting and revealing comments emerged.

"I didn't like to stare at another person for so long."

"I couldn't think of anything to tell."

"I said she had pretty hair and that she wore it well."

"I told him I liked his shirt."

---

[5] A booklet by Marshall Rosenberg is helpful in encouraging the "ability to recognize and verbally report feelings." See *A Manual for "Responsible" Thinking and Communicating* (St. Louis: Community Psychological Consultants, 1972), pp. 6-9.

action, reaction, and inaction

From the experience and the discussion, I believe a number of students realized as they never had before how (1) they were not used to noticing individual differences in others, and thus did not know how to go about it, (2) they tended to translate my request to "notice" into the threatening behavior of *staring*, thus becoming uncomfortable as both noticer and noticee, and (3) many of the individual "descriptions" were actually overt judgments or evaluations. Only a few people were comfortable focusing on such "noticings" as the color of eyes, the shape of the chin, the style of clothes.

Obviously, elements of evaluation will influence what we see and what we don't; there seems to be a certain inevitability to judgmental processes we cannot escape. Nevertheless, it was possible for the group to observe differences between those who "homed in" first on judgment or evaluation, and those who focused on the accuracy of what they observed rather than what they liked or inferred about what they observed.

Such judgmental tendencies, when directed at persons, almost always produce defensiveness. Students know this as well as anyone in our society, and better than most. Defensiveness assures distortion in communication.[6]

So I'd like to remind you that when you're tempted to judge or evaluate a person (teacher, administrator, fellow student, yourself), doing your perceptual homework means a commitment to accurate description. The description may be of your emotions, it may be of the other's behavior or appearance as you see it, it may be your perception of the relationship.

People's reactions are different when they see you as judgmental. They worry about whether you're trying to change them, whether you're in a campaign to shape them up. Most of us seem to resist actively this kind of relationship. Consider the following observation from Postman and Weingartner's *The Soft Revolution:*

> Ask a teacher, in a soft way, why he thinks some procedure he uses is good for students, and he will reply, "You mean, it isn't?" Ask in a hard way, and you get something different. Then, he will react the way most people do when they are unsure of themselves: He will rededicate himself to the behavior you challenged.[7]

Thus there is a special wisdom when we hear Estraven speak from the planet of Gethen in *The Left Hand of Darkness:*

---

[6] See Jack R. Gibb, "Defensive Communication," *The Journal of Communication,* 11 (September 1961), 141-148.

[7] Neil Postman and Charles Weingartner, *The Soft Revolution: A Student Handbook for Turning Schools Around* (N. Y.: Delta Books, 1971), p. 15.

students as real people

They say here "all roads lead to Mishnory." To be sure, if you turn your back on Mishnory and walk away from it, you are still on the Mishnory road. To oppose vulgarity is inevitably to be vulgar. You must go somewhere else; you must have another goal; then you walk a different road.[8]

Attempts at persuasion almost always increase resentment, defensiveness, and distortion. For these reasons I'm beginning to believe that those times when I consciously try to persuade others are probably (in the language of U. S. military policy) "counterproductive." The study of persuasion in the literature of communication behavior research has usually been the study of how one person or group attempts to change the attitudes and/or behavior of another person or group. And, indeed, this is the connotation presumed by most everyday usage; persuasion is something one does to another to change the other to fit the goals of the persuader.

Martin Buber's distinction between "imposition" and "unfolding" is relevant here. To him, the attitude of the persuader is the attitude of imposition, of deciding that one's own goals are superior to one's need to know the other's personness. He notes that to the propagandist, ". . . various individual qualities are of importance only in so far as he can exploit them to win the other and must get to know them for this purpose."[9] Persuading others is a form of disaffirmation, a presumption that my existence is superior to someone else's in some tangible way, else why should I try to change them as I would my wallpaper if it begins to displease me? Attempts to persuade in this view are objectifications of persons, and they are probably recognized as such at some level of the other's consciousness.

I don't want to imply that the process of persuasion—attitude change to meet goals—does not happen. It does; and people constantly change their attitudes and behavior as a result of each other.[10] We have to. But the conscious attempt to change another is both a drag on the growth of the relationship, and pragmatically ineffective. People change attitudes largely as a result of overt or covert personal choice, to facilitate meeting personal needs. If your messages supply me with new choices, you have helped me realize my potential, and persuasion has occurred because I've altered my world-view. I've changed me. But to contend

---

[8] Ursula K. LeGuin, *The Left Hand of Darkness* (N.Y.: Ace Books, 1969), pp. 146-147.

[9] Martin Buber, *The Knowledge of Man: A Philosophy of the Interhuman,* ed. Maurice Friedman (N. Y.: Harper Torchbooks, 1965), p. 82.

[10] Some communication theorists claim that all communication is ultimately persuasive. See James H. Campbell and Hal W. Hepler (eds.) *Dimensions in Communication: Readings* (Belmont, California: Wadsworth, 1965).

action, reaction, and inaction

"you've changed me" is not only inaccurate but conceptually misleading in its implication that there is some form of imposition of your will on mine.

According to Clark Moustakas' distinction,

> In the creative relationship changes occur not because one person deliberately sets out to influence and alter the behavior or attitude of another person but because it is inevitable that when individuals really meet as persons and live together in a fundamental sense they will modify their behavior so that it is consistent with values and ideals which lead to self-realizing ends. The creative relationship is an experience of mutual involvement, commitment, and participation, a meeting of real persons.[11]

Buber's notion of "unfolding" depends upon the ability of each of us to recognize that others necessarily develop their private and totally unique methods of coping with the world. No other way can be imposed upon the individual without a diminishing of his or her personness. But a different way can be unfolded, gently offered by any of us who have the courage to be educators. (All of us have the ability.) Growth is a natural force in persons, and the unfolding educator ". . . is confident that this growth needs at each moment only that help which is given in meeting, and that he is called upon to supply that help."[12]

The process of persuasion truly implies, then, not a propagandistic or manipulative relationship, but a helping relationship similar to that of the so-called "helping professions" of counseling and social work. The concept of "persuader"—whose responsibility (literally response-ability) is limited to implementing his or her goals through changing the other— is replaced by the concept of "helper"—whose response-ability is directed toward his or her understanding of and respect for the perspective and the worth of the other. This empathic direction is aided by nothing as much as persistent and responsible description and awareness of what *is*.

You-as-student can be this helper for those around you—other students, teachers, administrators. Helping is not role-bound. Describe the school to me. Describe me to me. Help me to understand. What I'll begin to understand is your school, your me, and through that I'll understand you better. But I'd rather you don't try to persuade me, even if you disapprove of my actions, even if it's for my own good.

---

[11] Clark Moustakas, *Finding Yourself, Finding Others* (Englewood Cliffs, N. J.: Prentice-Hall, 1974), p. 112.

[12] Buber, p. 83.

students as real people

Since a helper must be a person, too, with values, needs, opinions, and priorities, he or she must face social controversies effectively. I am not suggesting you stand idly by, watching ugly and evil conditions deteriorate while you try to describe them away, passive and impotent. "Persuasion as a helping relationship" can be activated only by forceful "statement" skills. Just as the effective professional helper/therapist works for full disclosing participation in dialogue with a client,[13] so you are able to work as a helper to change campus life just by stating what you believe to be true, and stating it where and when it will be heard.

I'm beyond pretending this isn't hard for students. The tendency seems to be for students either to suffer in silence under adverse educational conditions or (less commonly) challenge the source or messenger of those conditions aggressively in a sort of "you'd better change or else" persuasive attitude. Students appear to mirror communication habits of the general population concerning non-assertiveness and aggressiveness.

Most students entering college couldn't find a more useful book than *Your Perfect Right*, a brief but systematic introduction to assertive training by two psychologists.[14] Complete with examples and an agenda for changing behavior, this work seems important to me for two major reasons. First, it makes clear helpful distinctions between non-assertive, aggressive, and assertive behaviors. Briefly, understanding assertiveness allows one to speak up in explanation of his or her own rights or express personal wants without excessive anxiety. Non-assertiveness is characterized by high anxiety, a fear of honesty, a disrespect for one's own rights, and often, guilt feelings following the interaction for not saying what should have been said. Aggressiveness is demonstrated when the person speaks up to enhance himself or herself, but at the same time demeans the other's rights. The aggressive person views interaction as a battle to be won by defeating the other, the non-assertive person views interaction as just another occasion for losing, and therefore seeks not to participate. Only the assertive person has learned to view interaction in non-battle terms where both parties need to exercise interpersonal rights fully.

---

[13] See Sidney M. Jourard, *The Transparent Self* (rev. ed.; N. Y.: D. Van Nostrand, 1971), pp. 133-174; Carl Rogers, *On Becoming a Person* (Boston: Houghton Mifflin Sentry Edition, 1961), pp. 31-69.

[14] Robert E. Alberti and Michael L. Emmons, *Your Perfect Right* (2nd ed.; San Luis Obispo, California: Impact, 1974). I personally believe the issue of interpersonal rights in ongoing relationships is somewhat more situational than the Alberti and Emmons treatment seems to suggest. Most relationships become stronger, it seems, if participants do not assume rights are automatic possessions, but instead consider rights as behavioral agreements to be negotiated in dialogue. The genesis of interpersonal rights is not found in assumptions of universality, but talk in context.

action, reaction, and inaction

Few people would fit comfortably into just one of these broad categories. All of us can be expected to have exhibited each type of behavior at one time or another. Alberti and Emmons identify situational and generalized aspects of each of the three categories. For example, while those who behave typically non-assertively fit in the generalized non-assertive category, others who are confident and normally assertive in most encounters find themselves unable to assert their rights with some specific people or with some situations; these are the situationally non-assertive.

The second reason why *Your Perfect Right* seems so important for students is its affirmation that personal change in attitude can come from changes in behavior. Attitude change does not inevitably precede behavior change;[15] systematically trying out new behaviors can produce profound changes in attitude, but the commitment to the behavior experimentation must be sincere. This has enormous implications for the student situation, since it allows a breaking into the all-too-common cycle of self-deprecation and role anxiety. Acting assertively in appropriate situations, asserting rights, might not be found to be as dangerous as was assumed before the behavior change.

> We find the cycle can be reversed, becoming a positive sequence: more adequately assertive (self-enhancing) behavior gains more positive responses from others; this positive feedback leads to an enhanced evaluation of self-worth ("Wow, people are treating me like a worthwhile person!"); and improved feelings about oneself result in further assertiveness.[16]

In other words, you don't have to wait until your self-concept is strengthened significantly before you confront your advisor, assertively emphasizing your desire to schedule the courses that fit your personal or academic interests and requirements. Asserting will itself tend to improve your self-assessment.

If the idea of assertive training interests you, you might also want to investigate an analagous book combining some of the same background thinking with the concept of synergy.[17] James and Marge Craig observe that though many people are afraid of or mystified by power because exercising it seems to involve tangible rewards, punishments, and coercions, power can also come simply from showing others how to cooperate effectively toward common ends. Thus their scheme involves

---

[15] Ibid., p. 33.

[16] Ibid., p. 34.

[17] James H. Craig and Marge Craig, *Synergic Power: Beyond Domination and Permissiveness* (Berkeley: Proactive Press, 1974).

107

students as real people

distinguishing states of (1) no power (permissiveness), (2) directive power (domination), and (3) synergic power. They illustrate with the following, a "power triangle."[18]

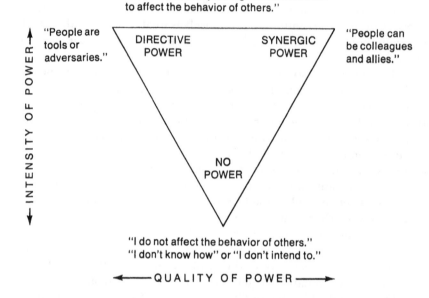

As with the non-assertive person who ignores the power of simple honest statement, Craig and Craig note that "probably the hardest person of all to move is the one stuck at the bottom of the power triangle—stuck because he/she believes it's wrong to try to intentionally affect the experience or behavior of others."[19] Students who are not treated as real people find it easy to believe this, becoming convinced that their role is so small and insignificant that to attempt to influence the system would be presumptuous. In asking you to consider forsaking persuading others, I could not ask you to avoid affecting them by acting intentionally. Effective people have effects on others—it's as simple as that.

Substituting the idea of statement for the idea of persuading others depends on some other factors explained in Chapter 5. Primarily, it involves your willingness to take responsibility for your own perceptions and feelings through "I-messages":

"I would rather have bought a different book for history, since this one seemed boring to me," not "You chose a lousy book."

"I am angry," not "You made me angry."

---

[18] Ibid., p. 64.

[19] Ibid., p. 65.

action, reaction, and inaction

"I really respond well to your teaching style," not "You're a great teacher."

"I was in the wrong mood today for that secretary's humor," not "She is really a bitch."

Prepare yourself for something, though. No matter how careful you are in disagreements to describe with I-messages instead of judge, some people will still perceive you to be judging and attacking. No matter how often you tell yourself you are not responsible for another's feelings, and that you must say what you must say, some people will still insist that you've "hurt them," or "broken their hearts." And no matter how clearly you believe you've tried to state your own, *owned,* perceptions, some people will still perceive you to be trying to change them. And no matter how much you feel affronted by another's behavior, asserting your rights then and there may be met with sanctions you don't want to have to deal with. So I'm not going to tell you these suggestions should be applied indiscriminately. I'm saying the opposite; if the consequences seem to be negative, you've got some weighing to do, and it's you that must do it, not me. Unfortunately, assertive, responsibility-taking statements are still too rare in our society for others to respond unwaveringly to an invitation to responsible dialogue where no one loses.

Option 4
Be in Class

Attending class is not the same as being in class. Every school has formulated a policy on attendance, most requiring it in some obvious or perhaps subtle way. The Faculty Handbook at SIUE, for example, reports that though there is no official university policy on "cuts," all faculty are supposed to keep careful attendance records and report to the administration those students who have missed three consecutive classes. Though nobody I know actually complies with this directive, the intent is pretty clear. Each teacher has formulated an attendance policy also, most requiring it with some vigor.

Although others can try to force you to attend class, no one can force you to "be" there, as a person. Classes I disliked or merely disdained were occasions for my academic automatic pilot to take over, a kind of inner robot I'd trained to take notes or occupy a seat without the slightest disturbance to where *I* wanted to be in my mind. Most of you have probably heard of the research project which discovered that of the students present at a series of university lectures, twenty per cent could be expected at any given moment to be thinking about sex.

I don't want to criticize the importance of sex, or its educational value, for that matter. The research results may have even been unduly influenced by the content of the lectures themselves, or the corny jokes

109

students as real people

sometimes thought to enhance them. Nevertheless, I must wonder, thinking back, how many of the lectures I ignored offered dialogue to which I was deaf. Opportunities were offered which were lost because *I* wasn't offering any. How many lectures were confusing to many of us when my question might have placed them in some perspective? How many discussions were flat because I, and others like me, didn't express disagreement with an interpretation because it was never really heard?

Oh, well. These have to remain rhetorical questions, I suppose, but it might profit you to ask some of them of your own behavior. Believe this; I have a lot of sympathy for the teacher of sculpture (true story) who just gave up addressing his class as a whole "because they pay no attention to anything not said to each personally."[20]

Option 5
Supply Your Own Reasons
A simple skill in theory: don't buy anyone else's reasons for your behavior. The only way really to own something is to make it yourself, and continually remake it, use-full and reason-able. Nobel prize-winning biologist George Wald believes supplying reasons to be the criterion of humanness:

> Animals for the most part do the right deeds, because they must to have survived, because they are made that way. They act ceaselessly, but in silence. They offer us no reasons.
>
> It is only man who accompanies every action with an explanation. He is forever talking, telling all who will listen just why he is doing whatever he does. It is plain enough that frequently the reasons he gives are improvisations, altogether suspect; but real or illusory, there are always his reasons.[21]

You tune into the sounds of self merging and emerging when you supply your own reasons. I see it so clearly now as I listen to my son Eric (five years old as I write this) who must maintain a running commentary on his experience. Every detail of a painting on the wall is described, every explanation for why he sees pirates in a seafood restaurant (yesterday, in a raucous tone), every reason for why I chose one meal and he another. I bristle in public partly because I'm in a sense more numb, certainly in a literal sense more dumb, less of a learner—and this contributes to my embarrassment more than I'm willing to admit on the spot. Frankly, I'm

---

[20] Jacques Barzun, *The American University: How It Runs, Where It is Going* (N. Y.: Harper Colophon Books, 1970), p. 209.

[21] George Wald, "On the Human Condition," *In the Name of Life: Essays in Honor of Erich Fromm*, ed. Bernard Landis and Edward S. Tauber (N. Y.: Holt, Rinehart and Winston, 1971), p. 112.

action, reaction, and inaction

somewhat out of the habit of commenting on my existence, explaining my perceptions to myself.

You might implement this option while considering any school assignment. Try supplying answers for yourself through questions like these:

"I'm staying up late tonight, studying this chapter on communication. What else could I be doing with this time? How will I feel in the morning? How crucial is my exam score? Am I reading differently than if a friend suggested the chapter? Than if I chose the book for my personal improvement? What are those differences? How can I personalize this *to me* when it was written ten years ago and two thousand miles away from now and here? Where do I go from now, where from here?"

Out of answers to these questions will emerge reasons. Reasons are doubly important because they glue your past to your future; they explain what you've done, describe what you're doing, and motivate what you will do. This is why "doing the right thing for the wrong reason" is so personally evil—it forms an historical discontinuity. There's no place to go, no forward reach to existence. No flow.

Terry Borton suggests a "What? So What? Now What?" instructional sequence for the humanistic teacher,[22] implementing the triad of historical process of past, present, future. Out of such questions reasons are supplied. I suggest the same approach for students confronting the size, complexity, and often impersonality of educational institutions.

Which leads to . . .

Option 6
Have Questions and Ask Questions

Few would challenge that the basic unit of formal education is the question. The question directed at you. Not the question springing spontaneously out of dialogue, not the inquiry, but the dare. The question aimed at you "for your own good," demanding proof that you've learned to use your mind, as Michael Rossman puts it, as a knife, " . . . to analyze and dissect, to fragment and divide, to distinguish cases with rational logic."[23]

Scenario: "Well, class, that's all we have time for today. The French Revolution will have to wait until Wednesday. Any questions? If not, I'll certainly have some for you on Friday! Be sure to review chapters eight to eleven." Nervous smiles at the tired joke. Shuffling and scuffling, crowding the double doors en route to a quick lunch or Geography lab.

---

[22] Terry Borton, *Reach, Touch, and Teach: Student Concerns and Process Education* (N.Y.: McGraw-Hill, 1970), Chapter Seven.

[23] Michael Rossman, *On Learning and Social Change* (N. Y.: Random House, 1969), p. 161.

students as real people

Face it. You aren't often expected to have questions. You aren't expected to ask them. A student once told me of a professor who was tape recording his lectures either for the general enlightenment of posterity or for preparation of a scholarly book. Anyway, this man would tolerate no interruptions at all, much less questioning. Before students discovered the full meaning of this, one poor soul raised her hand and repeated "Dr. Smith . . . Dr. Smith . . . Dr. Smith . . ." several times with rising volume, perhaps thinking the man was hard-of-hearing. When he could tolerate the interruption no more, "Dr. Smith" clicked off his tape recorder, perfunctorily answered, pressed the rewind button to the sentence preceding her first attempt to gain his attention, and repeated into the microphone the sentences his audience had already heard, this time without interruption.

The monologue was probably uninterrupted for the rest of the course.

Most instructors in my experience are not as insulated and unresponsive as "Dr. Smith." Most, I've found, welcome the idea of responding to questions after they've convinced themselves that meaningful questions are forthcoming. But almost nothing deflates me more as a teacher than to finish expressing what I consider to be a rare and profound insight, inquire about students' responses or questions, and hear only, "do you want the papers single-spaced or double-spaced?"

Asking me questions which invite comparison of our individualized reasons can convince me in a way no other action can that you're serious about your education. Having questions and asking them is a further skill you can use to break into a self-sustaining cycle of monologue and complaint.

I'm hoping Chapter 6 was helpful in presenting ways to ask orienting questions of your environment. Your skill in doing that combined with your courage to confront teachers and administrators with statements of your reasons and inquiries about theirs, will determine your receptivity to this next action alternative.

Option 7
Investigate the System Thoroughly

I suppose most students I know can identify the name of their college president; but not many are even remotely aware of which decisions around campus come (or can come) from his or her office. Most know what the University Senate is; not many know how much power it has. Most know that there is a system of academic tenure (not "ten-year" as a student once interpreted it) whereby faculty are kept on a probationary status for several years; but few are aware of what criteria are taken into account in the granting of tenure, or how this pressure affects

112

action, reaction, and inaction

the classroom behavior of their instructors. Most know there is a university budget carefully prepared; few know how that pie gets sliced, and therefore most get a thin slice. Most have grievances; few know there are places to take them for a hearing.

None of this information is secret. Gaining it is more a question of student motivation than access, though, in fact, it's vital to your education.

Though it's easy to exist day to day with your book reports, texts, and exams, the university offers an exciting laboratory in which to study "real life" in action. I'm getting tired, frankly, of hearing the student complaint of having to bide time in school until one can enter the "real world." Then students plunge headlong into the "real world" of IBM or General Motors, bewildered by the monstrous bureaucracy and unable to deal with it, frustrated at being treated like an expendable pawn. What's unreal about the school you attend except for students' inclination to withdraw unwisely but without much retribution from its internal workings? Bureaucracies are bureaucracies.

Knowing how the place works is important in separating the actors from the reactors, the doers from the done-to. But there are no courses in this. The institution doesn't tell you that this question of finding out about your education *is* your real education for a real world, in a real world.

Thus, students often don't realize that the next option is available in any meaningful sense.

Option 8
Commit Yourself Responsibly to Campus Decisioning Processes
You make a place for yourself in the social sense (and a place for your self in a personal one) by *doing*. After the reasons, questions. After questions, investigation. After investigation, involvement. No other paradigm makes as much sense.

But participation in campus governance is the reasonable but unfulfilled "now what?" of the post-sixties college population. After a flurry of activist student involvement in governance in the late sixties and early seventies, many people seemed to become disillusioned with the consequences and the effort expended. Even at the height of the involvement trend, and at relatively innovative liberal arts colleges, negative reports were noted similar to this dean's statement: "Student pressure to participate in college governance is increasing slightly, but our experience has been that relatively few students are willing to really do the work."[24]

---

[24] Michael Brick and Earl J. McGrath, *Innovation in Liberal Arts Colleges* (N. Y.: Teachers College Press, Columbia University, 1969), p. 84.

students as real people

According to another dean, though the faculty invited students to serve as voting members of the faculty Committee on Admissions and Student Aid, they ". . . have expressed preference for forgoing such participation, chiefly on the ground that they cannot spare the time that would be required."[25]

Arguments against a student voice in academic governance seem to rely on this observation; that students will not devote sufficient time or energy to the task. Why, they ask, do so few take even the trouble of voting in student government elections if this is not evidence of a lack of commitment? And we catch a glimpse again of the cyclic nature of expectation; students who are not expected to have effective contributions to make probably will avoid participation not because they can't, contribute but simply because they won't. (Often students who do choose participation do so only to gird themselves with data for future resumes, often alienating faculty and administrators by their low commitment.) Opponents of student governance power are thus given added ammunition for their arguments. A president of Cornell once remarked, ". . . a student is a student. He is at the university to learn, not to manage; to reflect, not to decide; to observe, not to coerce."[26]

Again, only student action can break into the cycle creatively and effectively. Others cannot legislate you into responsibility.

Two other arguments often prevail over increased student governance: first, "students are immature and are lacking in experience appropriate to such responsibilities," and second, "they have a short-term connection with the college, which means that present action does not carry with it subsequent responsibility."[27]

Certainly, I have noticed some immature students. Curiously, I notice more of them during times when I act immaturely. The question of experience is another matter entirely, one which a recent personal experience might illuminate. I had been asked by the New Student Life office on our campus to speak with a group of incoming freshmen about the nature of the campus and what range of experiences they might have in the classroom. Several of my former students were also present, as they were advisors in this program which orients new students to some valuable and available campus resources. During the give-and-take of questions and partial answers, I realized that I was sorely unprepared to answer questions about grading practices, actual attendance expectations, amount of written work, ratio of objective to essay tests, faculty

---

[25] Ibid.

[26] Paul Woodring, *The Higher Learning in America: A Reassessment* (N. Y.: McGraw-Hill, 1968), p. 145.

[27] Brick and McGrath, p. 84.

action, reaction, and inaction

tolerance of disagreement and controversy, syllabi, and the like. I just didn't know enough details to generalize about courses other than my own, faculties other than my department, requirements other than Speech Communication's. But the advisors, many of them barely sophomores, did. In a real sense, *they already had more relevant campus experience than I could bring into the group,* because their lives daily touched corners of the university I never explored.

All faculty in higher education must become, to a great extent, specialists. For administrators this is even more true. Students are generalists, though, and often admirably so. Because of the structure of our schools, student decision-making experience is often characterized by width rather than depth, but that is no one's fault, and is valuable experience nevertheless. Through exposure to this experience—really, only through exposure to it—the special interests of instructor and administrator gain perspective.

The observation that a student's connection with the institution is limited to a few years is true, but could translate into an advantage for a campus intelligent enough to encourage student governance procedures. Because of transitoriness, interests are less likely to become vested, special interest power bases less likely to become entrenched. Remember that students in governance usually work alongside other campus groups; the lack of student permanence is hardly going to cripple a university-wide committee. More likely it will periodically invigorate it with fresh perceptions, new ways of looking at old problems.

Mainly, though, student participation in campus governance provides a means of students and faculty getting together outside of the classroom, and another channel for the so-called "upward communication" so stressed in organizational theory. To one well known administrator, "The most successful arrangements for bringing students into communication with and influence upon university policy in its more critical areas of student relationships appear to be through . . . multiconstituent committees."[28]

In response to this realization and in recognition of some potential problems of student time and commitment for the effective operation of such committees, educator Earl McGrath has suggested a system of academic credit granted for student participation in governance.[29] McGrath's conclusions are noteworthy for both the dubious administrator and the uninvolved student:

---

[28] J. Douglas Brown, *The Liberal University: An Institutional Analysis* (N. Y.: McGraw-Hill, 1969), p. 87.

[29] Earl J. McGrath, *Should Students Share the Power?* (Philadelphia: Temple University Press, 1970), p. 98.

115

students as real people

> . . . thoughtful persons are convinced that the students' views on the changes that need to be made in American society and in higher education must be brought into official discussions of academic bodies, not as the recommendations of outsiders or supplicants, but as the expression of regularly constituted members of a community who have a right to participate in the activities of their government.
>
> Where students have been fully involved in academic government, they have typically discharged their responsibilities with effectiveness and with dignity.[30]

Higher education outside of the classroom is thus a clear option for you, one in which you can both implement and supplement your classroom learning.

P. S. . . .

I generated a lot of consciousness, I think, during a period in which most of what I've just written about alternatives for action would be labeled as hopelessly and oppressively "establishment." I'm a little sensitive to that, and uncomfortable encouraging others to consider participating when, for them, such "governance" may be sham if the institution merely sanctions the mechanism for, but does not listen to, student participation. You have to use your own judgment; I just hope you don't cop out on it.

Several authors who have my sympathy when they despair of American higher education—including Jerry Farber in *The Student as Nigger,* Michael Rossman in *On Learning and Social Change,* and Robertson and Steele in *The Halls of Yearning*—would doubt that perpetuating outmoded and basically authoritarian modes of academic decisioning provides any answer at all. They and others have suggested more radical actions such as strikes, obstructions, confrontations, and more important, open-ended, ad hoc networks of communication and cooperation. Entrenched system rigidity does need to be shaken up at times; such shocks redirect energies and free imaginations, if only momentarily. The turmoil of the sixties was probably inevitable, and probably helpful in the long run. But its intensity could/should not have been maintained. It burned white hot, scorched the scorchable, enlightened the willing, and warmed the vision. It supplied a new sense of what is possible, but supplied as well a renewed fear that the system's covert silent violence to

---

[30] Ibid., p. 105.

action, reaction, and inaction

the human spirit when met by revolutionary destructive violence to the property and sensibility of the "establishment" is still too much violence.

The enthusiasm for personal growth and community connection prevalent now in many students represents for me a more affirming and ultimately more realistic approach to social change in this age. I believe these persons seek a learning community where they can respond to diversity, where they can learn by the realistic, caring interaction of subcultures. And, by and large, I believe they are finding it by doing it.

appendices

I wrote the letters of Appendices A and B to participants in intensive five day workshops in interracial communication conducted in the summers of 1975 and 1976 at Southern Illinois University at Edwardsville. I have mixed feelings about including them here, since I've had second thoughts about some of the things written in the letters. I've resisted the temptation to "clean them up," though, and they are reproduced here with no substantial changes. These messages to students provide artifacts of my feelings at these two important times in my life, and indications of how it was for groups to try to implement some ideas of this book.

Finally, I've decided to include as Appendix C the current description for my sections of the basic interpersonal communication course at SIUE. Maybe this, too, will help you understand the connection I affirm between education and communication. I hand it out on the first day of class, and hope it has for students the tone of invitation. It's ironic but somehow appropriate that an introductory invitation concludes the book. The longer I live, the more I see that most things are inviting, and each thing I learn is merely an invitation to another learning. The title of poet John G. Neihardt's autobiography is always with me: "All is but a beginning."[1]

---

[1] John G. Neihardt, *All Is But a Beginning: Youth Remembered, 1881-1901* (N. Y.: Harcourt Brace Jovanovich, 1972).

appendices

Appendix A (1975)

As I'm starting to confront my blank sheet of paper, I'm pretty unsure of where this letter should start and even less sure of where it should go.

My first impulse is to start with a justification of how and why I decided to orient the workshop toward the direct experience of interracial communication rather than a more traditional emphasis on "cognitive" learning or specific skill acquisition. Several of you, I feel, would like to discuss this with me, and I'd like that, too. But most of you seem pleased with the opportunity for dialogue in an unrestricted atmosphere; pleased with the idea that we, working together, could "make" the class. So I'm fighting my defensiveness and "teacherish" tendencies to explain when no further explanation is probably necessary.

How well did we do together? I'm not sure as I write this (Thursday night). We still have a day to go. And, as it's said that dying people see their lives flashing before them, perhaps on the last day of our dispersing group, our history will flash a new insight or two for me. Hope so. Right now my feeling is primarily positive. I'm happy we happened.

On Monday I was surprised at how quickly and clearly the group led into its own transitions, established its own norms, and diversified its own functioning. If a bunch of people is to transform itself into a community, it must find a way to become self-regulating and self-adjusting. I saw the beginnings of this Monday and the flowering of it this afternoon when we let ourselves do something difficult to justify on an "accountability/efficiency" basis, simply to talk informally in small groups for two hours *at no one's specific suggestion*. Frankly, I was tired of initiating action and was curious to see what would happen if I didn't. Several of you looked uncomfortable, but might not have believed it was a realistic choice for you to initiate or suggest. I find that reluctance unfortunate (if it existed), but it seemed to me the group as an organism wanted "breathing space." Despite the camps of agreement and disagreement within the group and the high emotional involvement of the majority of the members, we cooperated so consistently on procedures throughout the week that it seems unlikely it was an accident. I've been in a lot of groups, but rarely have seen this phenomenon.

Two other factors appear to be important in communities, too, and I believe we hit on one while not completely fulfilling the other. First, communities are groups in which individuals are noticed and taken into account. In a true community, people are aware of your absence and you're missed. I felt good about my sense of who was "with" the group, physically and psychologically, and who we were "missing," physically and psychologically.

students as real people

The final idea of community I want to mention, though, is not as encouraging to me. A community should be a place in which it's ok to make a mistake. If I'm a member of a true community, I'm constantly risking myself because I'm constantly accepted and affirmed despite my increased vulnerability and perhaps even despite my increased foolishness. (I now am writing from Sunday's perspective.) I saw a lot of risks taken during the week to which many reacted with appreciation and empathy. Some were mine. I tried to be as fully "with" the group as I could; but I never rid myself of the fear that there were certain expressions and feelings which were permissible to share with blacks and others which were taboo. If I've had black friends in the past, for example, how am I to draw on this experience in the group without mentioning it? And how do I mention it without violating the expressed desire of some blacks not to hear whites say such clichéd and transparent things? I was pleased that we discussed this problem on Friday; I felt better than I had on Wednesday and Thursday about it. Another example: I am often hopelessly confused about the origin and nature of my prejudice. Several times I heard blacks suggest there were concealment motives behind whites' inability to be specific in response to the (admittedly) more vivid openness of the group's blacks. Soon I became afraid of and defensive about revealing my uncertainty for fear it immediately would point to my insincerity. I know many whites do not understand the fear and resentment in blacks as a result of a racist society; but I'm only newly aware that many blacks do not understand the disorientation and bewilderment of well-meaning whites raised in the same racist society. And this frustrated me as much as anything during our week together.

But overall, I learned too much with you to be disappointed with the experience. I learned how much my own baggage interferes with my responding to you spontaneously in our present. I learned that my well-meaning facade of not expressing anger toward blacks does me no good and might even foster the growth of more destructive facades. I learned that my fear of many aspects of black culture might not be as great as my jealousy of the community/identity spirit of much of that culture. But both the fear and the jealousy probably contribute to my prejudice.

Most of all I've learned that the idea with which I started this week has a good deal of validity. I told you Monday this was my first experience with a group like this, but that despite my nervousness I felt that interracial communication didn't have to depend on a separate bag of gimmicks and techniques. Instead, the general ideas of effective interpersonal communication are applicable.

I find it encouraging to affirm that strong interracial relationships can be facilitated by nothing more complicated than sincere people interacting over time with just a few mutual agreements about format. At

appendices

the beginning of the week I was prepared to provide us with a large number of structured activities which led to "conclusions" about communicating. I now feel we didn't need them and am pleased with myself for not forcing them on us. The behaviors and response styles which would have been realized by these activities largely evolved from our group *anyway*: an "I-orientation," a "problem-orientation," the notion that honesty and trust are options in interracial relationships, the process of active and affirming listening, the analysis of "baggage," a "here-and-now orientation," non-judgmentalism, the idea that others do not exist to be "changed," the positive results of intergroup conflict, the idea that only through risk will my boundaries and your meanings become clearer to me.

In other words, I've learned that contact helps, and that conflict helps. Through contact and conflict can come connection—even when resentments and confusions are deep and intense. Thanks for your help.

Hope to see you soon. . . .

Love,
Rob

Appendix B (1976)

Believe it or not, slicing doctors, nosey nurses, and boring TV could not take my mind off the group; I'm still carrying you all around with me. It's not easy for me to get either into *or* out of such an intensive experience.

Reading your exams and (especially) letters has reaffirmed my belief that this experience absorbed incredible commitment from individuals in the group. Of course, your perceptions of the meaning of it all were so different that it's hard to generalize, and really impossible to summarize "how it went" for someone who wasn't there. This is interesting to me—this process of trying to explain an intensive group to a non-member. Perhaps you experienced the same thing. Several "outsiders" approached me during the week and good-naturedly inquired how we were doing. I inevitably had to answer how *I* was doing.

I just noticed how neatly this idea fits into our theme of *personal awareness of personal differences* as the key to interracial communication.

Anyway, I thought that since you were kind enough to share your letters with me, I should share one with you. I want you to know what I learned or reaffirmed in our week together.

—I learned again how important it is that we take every opportunity to interact when our topic is really also our process. Our time together could have been "cognitive" and fact-centered; or could have been more issued-centered (should we bus more school children? Estab-

students as real people

lish more hiring quotas?) But, by and large, we can inform ourselves by ourselves with books (prisoners in solitary confinement read a lot), and we—in CB 2042—aren't going to shape up Boston, East St. Louis, or IBM. I feel strongly that in beginning social change, I have to start with me and we have to start with us. Perhaps change will occur in others by their noticing mine. Perhaps not. No guarantees. Consistently, though, my best learning (i.e., changing) experiences have been those in which I've been free to try out behaviors in unexplored directions that look pretty good to me.

—I learned in new ways that one of the most crucial variables in group work is the extent to which individual wants are verbalized. I can't find any value in an experience until I put something of value into it. My negative reactions are of value to you; when I withhold them, I withhold part of my commitment to making the group work. Not surprisingly, then, the group works less well, and my dissatisfactions multiply. Remember Jim Craig's short essay on the yellow-sheet handout?

—I learned how angry some could be under a usually-calm exterior. I sometimes forget. Thanks for shaking me up.

—I learned I very often choose to ride on the waves of other people's emotions and behaviors. When you were bored, I sometimes yawned, too. When you were excited and involved, my spirits lifted, too. When you were critical and demanding, I tended to get contentious. Don't much like this in me, but it's there—and I really felt it strongly during our week together.

—I learned how tentative and unsettled I still am in my "role" in the group. Clues: my defensive explanation of why I was the group "leader" instead of an interracial team. I still tend to take too much responsibility for what's going on (I'm better at this than I used to be). I sometimes took it personally when some of you were not in the room at the agreed time (especially Friday morning). I summarized very selfishly at times. Oh, well.

—I learned how coalitions and subgroups don't need to form along racial lines in such a group. In fact, during our week, they rarely did. Why did this surprise me?

—I reaffirmed that individual awareness and descriptive tendencies are probably the key skills in interracial understanding. From them, empathy can develop; without them, it's futile. Interracial communication is tough. Takes a lot of commitment for me to see the differences between you and not-you. I lose track of that commitment at times.

—I found out again how hard it is for me to do what I told you was most important, to trust the process of sincere people doing the best they could to understand (not change) each other. I think some of you found that it was *too* hard and bailed out, frustrated that the group didn't communicate the way you would if you were simultaneously everyone

122

appendices

else. If that was you, you missed a lot. For although many of you didn't always use the terminology *I'd* have chosen, and though many interruptions irritated *me,* and though some of you didn't seem to be listening when *I* thought it important, I still learned a hell of a lot by not turning you off and throwing up my hands in despair.

Finally, a couple of thoughts I had as a result of the workshop:

Yeah you're black
And I'm afraid of the steps of
My speech—
Tentative words
Tip-toeing through
Trembling lips
With fear I'll offend
Not to be cruel
But to be not cool.

Yeah I'm white
And I'm afraid of the brass of
Your speech—
Blunt bright
Bowl 'em over bravado
Betcha can't top this
And I don't
Because I can't?
Because I won't?

Yeah we're different
I can tell even over the phone
If I'm quiet enough I hear
My fears plainly
And if I'm just a bit more quiet
Your fears might come through too.

We spent a week together
And you ask
What was the
Experience worth?
Well I say
I was wondering
What the experience
Was

students as real people

Could it be
Our separate questions were
Only one
Rephrased?

Our experience
Was worth
What it *was*
Period

And
As we just notice
Notice what it was
Together

Describing focusing co-focusing
We value it highly
Indeed

But when we
Walk away
Frightened of phrasing
Our own descriptions
Even to ourselves
The experience
Cheapens

Accurate description may be
Our most courageous
Personal and interpersonal
Act

Love,
Rob

Appendix C (1977)

To Students in GSK 123, "Oral Communication of Ideas"
Rob Anderson

"I have been attending SIU for 3+ years. I have never tried to really talk with another person. I have been a robot coming to school, going to class, taking notes, and going home. I digest what's been given to me and spit out the info in hopes of a good grade. Now at least through the impact of this class I am trying to get into

appendices

communication with others in some of my classes and it's working. The robot is becoming human. See, I'm not really a robot elsewhere. I was just so concerned with coming to school to get the grades and get out of school. I felt no need for any personal interactions with others. I only wanted an education. Now I think that maybe the reason I quit SIU (for two years) was because I helped create this coldness. I always thought it was SIU and its hassles—now I think part of the problem was me. I was expecting to attend X number of hours at SIU and never get involved. You can't do this and expect to enjoy any of it."

Debbie Lacquement
GSK 123, 1976

"To You.
Stranger, if you passing meet me and desire to speak to me, why should you not speak to me?
And why should I not speak to you?"

Walt Whitman, 1860

"Clean your window or I'll only see your pane."

Biff Rose, 1969

"The quality of our interpersonal relationships determines who we are becoming as persons. Interpersonal communication is not just one of many dimensions of human life; it is the defining dimension, the dimension through which we become human."

John Stewart and
Gary D'Angelo 1975

I'd like for you to read this "syllabus" as an invitation to participate with me in determining the nature of our class. It is not predetermined. We have a lot of decisions to make.

There is not one set of Answers I have in mind for you to learn. Answers are personal; I can share some of mine, but you have to develop your own for learning to be meaningful. The format of the class presumes:
(a) students care strongly about their education;
(b) students have a lot to teach each other; and
(c) the notion of communication effectiveness has a high degree of transfer to the rest of the educational process.

You have the potential to expand greatly your range of insights into problems of interpersonal communication and their possible solutions. Hopefully, you will take out of the course the habit of responding to

students as real people

these problems with sound judgment and "opening" behavior. But I need to say, though, that while GSK 123 classes often interact readily and satisfyingly, they can also develop apathy, hostility, and/or competitiveness. In this regard, the class is similar to most other human groups; your observation of its behavior and your transactions with it become the main concerns of the course. The textbook is only meant to be an idea-stimulant. *You* are the content of this course.

If You'd Like to Talk with Me Outside Class:
My office is 2107 Rendleman Building. You can stop by there any time you want, but if you'd rather set up a specific time to meet, you could call 692-3090 (the office phone) or my home, 656-5627. I don't mind being called at home.

I've found that instead of "office hours," I see a lot more people—and enjoy seeing them more—by being in the Goshen Lounge for four hours or so a week at a set time (or outside the Center if it's a nice day). This quarter I'm there at these times, barring emergencies:—————
————————.

Text:
Stewart and D'Angelo, *Together: Communicating Interpersonally*

I believe the organization of this book can easily become the organization for our course. The authors start with a clear statement of the importance of interpersonal communication, then build on it skillfully. I recommend you read the chapters in sequence. You might find that *Together* has a different "feel" than any other textbook you've ever read —Stewart and D'Angelo seem real, and human.

Expectations:
Journal. Keep a journal of communication perceptions of our class and your feelings about those perceptions. During the process of writing about your ideas and feelings, you'll find yourself (I hope) thinking about them more, considering them more carefully, thinking them through more clearly, perhaps, than before. Keeping a journal is an important learning experience. Make an entry for each class period. (If you want to write about out-of-class experiences, that would be nice, too.) Watch especially for evidence of growth or decay in relationships, listening behavior, openness, attempts at persuasion, your self-concept and how it's affected by communication, etc. Your first tendency (if you're like me) will be merely to describe what's going on, while neglecting to report how you feel about the situations. However, since this is a

appendices

personal journal, try to let the focus be on your emotional reactions to events at the time you're writing (hopefully soon after the events described). Journals obviously don't have to be polished literary documents. *Most important,* you should know that: (a) this is *not* a graded assignment, nor will your comments affect the grades of others; and (b) that if you keep the journal confidential, showing it only to me, you can be as candid and personal as you wish. Needless to say, I will keep the journals totally confidential. Toward the end of the quarter, I'll ask you to turn yours in, and, if you wish, we can talk about your perceptions of the relationships you've developed. (Ungraded; prerequisite to completing the course)

Participation in Reaction Groups. Four groups will be formed in the first week of the course. They will meet at least once a week for the following purposes: (a) to consider class topics in a more intimate setting than is possible in a group of 30; (b) to allow a relatively nonthreatening climate for sharing new ideas and behaviors; (c) to provide feedback to me about the value and directions of the course, and (d) to coordinate group presentations during the last third of the quarter. Each group will have one class hour available, in which it can explain its experience to the rest of the class in a creative way, or creatively present the group's interpretation of a specific topic. (Ungraded; prerequisite to completing the course)

Choose Any Three of the Following Graded Projects:
Mid-term Exam. Any time from the fourth to the sixth week of class, you may request to take an essay exam of about two hours' duration, scheduled at your convenience. If enough people wish to take the exam, and we can agree on a time, I can schedule it during class time. Criteria for my reactions: (a) understanding of concepts; (b) application of concepts to daily-life situations. (Graded)

Personalizing a Book. You may choose any book which has contributed to your understanding of interpersonal communication and show how it affected you, uniquely and personally. I'm suggesting here that you go beyond a traditional "book report" to tell me (in 5-8 typewritten pages) something of *yourself as a communicator* using the book as a vehicle. (Graded)

Letting Your Philosophy Emerge. I believe each of us carries around a unique philosophy of communicating which we constantly act upon (and adjust, when necessary) relative to our relationships. But it's unusual and challenging to try to *notice* yourself in relationship, letting your

127

students as real people

philosophy emerge on paper (5-8 typewritten pages). As a suggested structure: write about your five most important learnings about communication. If they're consistent with the ideas of GSK 123, show how; if they seem contrary to course concepts, explain. (Graded)

Speaking With the Group. Choose one concept or idea from *Together,* and in 10-20 minutes, explain it and go beyond it creatively in an informal but prepared "speech" to the class. You may wish to add your own definitions, examples, resources, applications to life situations, etc. Schedule time for this with me whenever you like. (Graded)

Do you have another idea for an equivalent project? Let me know.

Conferences:
I'd like to talk with each of you individually in the first few weeks of the quarter, to get to know you better and sooner. Just an invitation.

And....
Attendance is optional in this class. You should be responsible for setting your educational priorities, and that includes deciding when it may be more important to do something else than to attend GSK 123. However, to be completely candid, I should mention that you may find it difficult to fulfill the journal and project expectations without the base of concepts and experiences provided by class discussions and activities. Also, I hope you do not consider attendance optional on those days when your group has a presentation, or you've scheduled a project.

I am most comfortable and learn best in informal situations. I'd like you to try to learn the names of everyone in class. Straight rows aren't required. You don't need to bother raising your hand when you want to say something. I've found that being known as "Rob" helps me feel more comfortable in the classroom situation. It's a small matter, but first names are much nicer and more personal.

Finally, a word (warning?) about my role in the class. Some of you who are used to and perhaps value highly structured, teacher-centered classes may be struck by what a poor "teacher" I am. I usually bring up more questions than I have answers for. Often, students in class talk more than I do. I often avoid advice, offering guidelines instead of positive answers. I almost never lecture, submitting to it only occasionally, and reluctantly. I make clear in class many of my personal prejudices and emotions and will supply lots more if you care to ask. I have been accused at times of sacrificing order and structure for chaos in my classes.

appendices

But it's easy for me to rationalize away those potential faults, since I am in agreement with psychologist Carl Rogers that "teaching" (in its most common definition) is a "vastly overrated function." It implies that I have sole possession of something I must give you—or force you to take—and that the only reason you are here is to get what I am paid to teach you. This write-it-fast-in-your-notebook model of education, though, negates most of what we will learn about human communication, and would be absurd in a communication class. If effective communication is two-way, then effective education must be two-way. I cannot just be a "teacher"—if we are to communicate, I must be a learner as well, since you all represent new experiences to me. You cannot just be passive learners—if we are to communicate, you must share something of yourself with the rest of us.

I am not above this process—I'm an unavoidable participant in it. What I can do is to help facilitate your learning (and mine) by encouraging us to experience firsthand the problems and successes of communication. What I want you to get is *your* education from this class, not *my* education warmed over.

(I guess the "syllabus" became your first long reading assignment. I'd be interested in your reactions to what I've suggested for our course.)

129

index

"Academic" student subculture, 88
Acceptance, 59–61, 96
  unconditional, 70
Acceptance education, 55
Active listening, 61–63
Agel, J., 14
Alberti, R.E., 106
Anchor, psychological, 12
Assertive training, 106–107
Assertiveness
  contrasted with nonassertive and
    aggressive behavior, 106–107
  and self-assessment, 107
Attendance, 128
  policy, 109
Attitude change, and disclosure, 66
Audience, 87–92
Audienceness, 73–75
Availability, 45
Awareness, of personal differences,
  121–122

"Baggage" and communication, 120–
  121
Baird, S., 100
Barbara, D., 52–53
Barker, L., 44
Barzun, J., 110
Bateson, G., 81
Beavin, J. H., 33
Be-ing, 96, 109–110
Bem, D., 66
Benedict, R., 77

Bodymind, 75
Borton, T., 111
Boulding, K., 28
Bradbury, R., 83
Brainstorming, 84
Brick, M., 113
Brown, C.T., 47, 67, 82
Brown, J. D., 115
Buber, M., 104–105
Butt, D. E., 94

Campbell, J. H., 104
Camus, A., 64
Carson, J., 24
Centering and self, 10
Challenge, attitude of, in listening,
  60
Change, as norm in communication,
  14
Chapin, H., 51
Chickering, A. W., 50
Choice, 54–55, 67
  as communication resource, 83
Choice-to-listen, 44
  and other-affirmation, 46–48
Clark, B. R., 88
"Collegiate" student subculture, 88
Committee on the Student in Higher
  Education, 18, 50, 98
Communication
  and interdependence, 4–5
  and relativity, 4
  as a "we-process," 22

130

index

Community, 96–101
  in classrooms, 99
  criteria, 97
  and current student attitudes, 117
  living-based, 98
  and mistakes, 120
  and noticing, 119
  and self-regulation, 119
  sense of, on campuses, 3
Compliance behavior, 94
Confirmation, 48
Conflict, 121
Confusion, as indicator of learning, 8
Craig, J. H., 55, 107–108, 122
Craig, M., 55, 107–108

Dahms, A., 89
D'Angelo, G., 125–126
Defensiveness, 103
Dialogue, 24–25, 102
  and learning, 36
Domination, 108

Ecology
  and communication environment,
    79–87
  student interest in, 80
Emmons, M. E., 106
Emotions
  and action on campus, 101–102
  and control, 10, 66–67
  and expectations of students, 17
  internal origins of, 9
  and rights in relationships, 64–65
  and wholeness in learning, 12–13
Empathy, 122
  and active listening, 62–63
  and listening, 44
Expectation, 15–20
  and college student behavior, 16–
    20
  impact of, 15–16

Faculty, attitudes toward teaching,
    90–91
Fantini, M. D., 63
Farber, J., 19, 100, 116
Farson, R., 61

Feedback, 68–69
  and dialogue, 25
  and the "Pygmalion effect," 15
Feit, K., 100–101
Fiore, Q., 14
Flexibility, as a root-resource, 81
Fox, A. V., 46
Friedland, W. H., 85
Fromm, E., 55, 62, 92
Fuller, R. Buckminster, 14, 76–77

Gardner, J. W., 34
Gauss, M., 73
Gibb, J. R., 56–57, 61, 84, 103
Gibb, L., 56
Ginott, H., 48
Goffman, E., 7
Goodman, P., 17, 89
Goodstein, L., 78, 88
Gordon, T., 48, 61
Governance, 97, 113–116
Grades, 9
  as artificial resources, 85
  as barrier to communication, 2
  and mistakes, 18

Hanna, T., 55
Harrison, R., 32
Hartford, J., 83
Hearing, distinguished from
    listening, 47
Heist, P., 88
Hepler, H. W.., 104
"Here-and-now orientation," 121
Horowitz, I. L., 85
Howe, L. W., 49
Hyams, E., 79, 81

I-messages, 68, 108–109
I-orientation, 121
Identity, 10–12
  and disclosure, 65–66
  and interaction, 19
Image, 28
"Imposition," 104
Interdependence
  in the communication
    environment, 83
  in TORI theory, 57
Interior regulation, 9–10, 17

131

students as real people

Interpersonal communication, 21
Interracial communication, 118–124
Invitation, attitude of, in listening, 60

Jackson, D. D., 33
Johnson, L., 65–66
Johnson, W., 66
Jones, J. E., 56
Joseph, S. E., 16
Jourard, S., 59, 106
Journal, 126
Judgment, 102–109, 121
  and listening, 61

Keen, S., 46–47, 70
Keller, P. W., 47, 67
Kelley, C. M., 44
Kelley, G, A., 35
Keltner, J., 45
Keniston, K., 7, 88
Kennedy, J. F., 12
Kilpatrick, W. Heard, 66
Kirschenbaum, H., 49

Lacquement, D., 125
Landis, B., 110
Learning
  act and attitude facets, 35
  built, not received, 36
  as caring, 38–39
  and the concept of person, 35
  and environment, 38
  and personal experience, 34–38
LeGuin, U., 88, 104
Leonard, G. B., 55
"License to disagree," 63
Listening, 121
  distinguished from hearing, 47
  functions of, 43–44
  importance in culture, 42–43
  and loneliness, 50–52
  as other-affirmation, 41–53
Love
  and orderliness in students, 18
  and trust, 59
Luft, J., 48, 64

Macrorie, K., 52
Manipulation, and students, 20

Marin, P., 17
Maslow, A., 77
Maturation, and individualization, 11
Mayeroff, M., 39
McGrath, E. J., 113, 115
McGuire, B., 2
McInnis, N., 18
Mead, G. H., 11
Metaperspectives, 29
Metzger, N. J., 94
Montagu, A., 11, 18
Moustakas, C., 105
Multilogue, 36

Neihardt, J. G., 118
No-fault communication, 25
"Nonconformist" student subculture, 88
Nonperson, 7, 21
Nonverbal communication, 30–33
Nyberg, D., 13

Oliver, R., 53
Openness, 59–71
  and availability, 46
  as a cycle, 67
  and disclosure, 63–71
  and receptivity, 59–63
  in TORI theory, 57
Opinions, as resources for learning, 81–83
Osborn, A. F., 84
Other-affirmation, 45

Perception, 15, 28–29
  and process, 26
  of relationships, 33
Permissiveness, 86, 108
Person, 6–21
  and choice, 94
  and communication, 6
  and the future, 55
Persuasion, 102–109
  as a helping relationship, 105–106
Pfeiffer, J. W., 56
Phillips, G. M., 94
Pollutants, in the communication environment, 86

index

Postman, N., 15, 103
Powell, J., 58–59
"Power triangle," 108
Powerlessness, and students, 20
Prather, H., 9–10
Problem-orientation, 121
Process, 26–28
    distinguished from events and
      objects, 13–14
"Pygmalion effect," 15

Question-ing, 111–112
Questions, in education, 70–71

Realization, in TORI theory, 57
Reason-ing, 96, 110–111
Reference groups, 15
Reich, C. A., 55
Relationship, and perception, 33
Reno, R. H., 25
Research, 96
Resources, as assumptions, 81
Response sets, 15
Responsibility, 105
    models in education, 39–40
Richards, A. C., 55
Richards, F., 55
Richards, M. C., 10, 14, 38, 93
Rights, interpersonal, 106
Robertson, D., 76, 89, 116
Rogers, C., 14, 48, 60–61, 106, 129
Roles, 57–59, 122
    and academic audiences, 73–74
Rose, B., 125
Rosenberg, M., 102
Rosenthal, R., 15
Rossman, M., 111, 116

Sandeen, A., 89
Scarcity assumption, 85
Schutz, W. C., 75
Seeman, M., 20
Self-disclosure, 35
    and emotions, 63–64
Self, discovery of, 10–11
Self-fulfilling prophecy, 15
Self-persuasion, 66
"Self-sphere" concept, 12
Sharing, 22

Simon, S., 49
Slater, P., 55, 85
Southern Illinois University-
    Edwardsville, 99–101, 109, 118,
    124–125
Statement skills, 102–109
Steele, M., 76, 89, 116
Stewart, J., 125, 126
Story, 46–47
Student culture, and listening, 49–53
Students
    activism and apathy, 71–72
    as generalists, 115
    subcultures
        see Subcultures, student
    as workers, 78
Subcultures, 19
    as communication phenomena, 89
    and expectations, 15
    student, 88–89
Symbolic communication, 30
Synergic power, 107–108
Synergy, 76–79, 107–108
Systems, approach to campus
    relationships, 75–76

Tauber, E. S., 110
Taylor, H., 49–50, 86, 92
Technology, 55
Telling, 9
Terry, M., 80
Thayer, L., 79–81
TORI, 56–59
Tournier, P., 33
Transaction, 29
Transactional analysis, 11
Trow, M., 88
Trust, 56–59, 121, 122
    and personal relationships, 8
    as prerequisite to effective
      relationships, 56

Unconditional acceptance
    see Acceptance, uncondi-
      tional
"Unfolding," 105

Values, 49
Van Riper, C., 82

133

students as real people

"Vocational" student subculture, 88
Voice, as communication resource,
83
Voting behavior, 15

Wald, G., 110
Wants, 122
Watzlawick, P., 33
Weaver, C., 43
Weaver, J., 78

Webster, H., 88
Weingartner, C., 15, 103
Weinstein, G., 63
Whitman, C., 51
Whitman, W., 125
Wholeness, 12–13, 96
Woodring, P., 114
Words, as symbols, 30

You-messages, 68